HOLES IN MY SHOES

OTHER BOOKS BY AUTHOR

Green Gravy, Monster Bread and Other Adventures

HOLES IN MY SHOES

One Family Survives the Great Depression

Alice Breon

Library of Congress Control Number:		2012915806
ISBN:	Hardcover	978-1-4797-0767-6
	Softcover	978-1-4797-0766-9
	Ebook	978-1-4797-0768-3

This book was printed in the United States of America.

To order additional copies of this book, contact:
Xlibris Corporation
1-888-795-4274
www.Xlibris.com
Orders@Xlibris.com

TO MY GREAT-GRANDCHILDREN

Bradley, Haley, Alyssa, Megan, Joshua, Matthew, Sarah, Courtney, Megan, Ryan, Tristan, Briana, Christopher, Madison, and those who are not here yet.

CONTENTS

PREFACE

Most people who are now in their '80s and '90s were children in the Great Depression. Among the people I interviewed for their memories of that era, there was one common theme. They all started out with, "We didn't know there was a Depression. Everyone was in the same boat."

Recycling and conservation are not new concepts to our generation. We lived it. We didn't know anything different. Leftovers were never discarded. They were used the next day in soups, hash, casseroles or salads. Milk and soda always came in glass bottles which were taken back to the store to be used again.

Women made dish cloths out of cloth feed bags. When there were holes in socks, they were mended until they were too threadbare to be mended. Then they were used as curlers. Damp hair was wrapped around the socks. When the hair was dry, the socks were pulled out, and perfect long curls were the beautiful result.

Disposable diapers had not yet been invented, so all diapers were made of cotton cloth and were laundered. Laundry was hung outdoors on lines for the sun and breeze to dry.

Recycling was our way of life. Not because of a desire to save the planet, but mostly because of necessity and partly because many things hadn't been invented yet.

And now, three generations later, we have the benefits of the great inventions that save time and energy. We can't even imagine what our dear descendants will develop to make the world better for their future generations, but the human spirit is resourceful, and ideas are abundant. I know they will come up with amazing results. I'd love to be around to see the changes.

THE DEPRESSION ARRIVES AT OUR HOUSE

Raggedy Andy lies crumpled on the dining room table. He is face down, legs splayed out in an uncomfortable position. His shirt and pants are missing. His red and white striped stockings and black shoes are all he has on.

What is he doing here? I had tucked him in his little bed beside Raggedy Ann last night before I went to sleep.

The year is 1931. I am six years old. I have many dolls in my bedroom upstairs, but the Raggedys were my favorites.

I found my mother at the kitchen sink washing the tiny shirt and pants. "Why are you washing Andy's clothes?" I asked. "We're going to visit Tommy and his mother this afternoon," she answered. Tommy was a three-year-old boy. Tommy and his mother were living with his grandparents.

My mother hung Andy's clothes outside to dry, and although my question hadn't been answered, I didn't pursue the subject. After lunch, my mother ironed Andy's clothes and dressed him while I changed into my "visiting clothes." She picked up Andy as we left the house, and I asked why Raggedy Andy was coming with us.

"Because we are going to give him to little Tommy," she explained.

"But he's *mine*!" I wailed.

"You have plenty of dolls, Alice. You should share with people who don't have as much as you have."

"But he belongs with *me*! And Raggedy Ann will miss him." This can't be happening. Surely my mother wasn't really going to give my doll away.

"Now, don't be selfish. We won't talk about it anymore."

We rode to Evanston in silence and I glanced occasionally at Andy who sat between my mother and me, looking handsome in his clean clothes. When my mother handed Andy to Tommy, I had my first experience of loss. The boy's happy smile and his mother's appreciation were of small comfort.

It was many years later when I understood why Andy had been taken from me so abruptly.

The stock market crashed in 1929. As a result, businesses closed, people lost their jobs, and there were no new jobs to be found. This period of time, from 1929 to 1939 was known as the Great Depression. My father designed and engraved fine gold jewelry. His jewelry was in great demand before the stock market crash, and our family lived in comfort.

By 1931, people were struggling to pay for food for their families. They had no money to buy fine jewelry, so my father's business dwindled.

He took part-time jobs in a post office and other places and managed to keep us fed. Luckily, he had paid for our house with cash when he bought it in 1921.

At the time of this story, Tommy's father had died suddenly of an illness. Tommy and his mother went to live with his grandmother who was my mother's friend.

My mother wanted to give the little boy something to play with but she had no money to spend on gifts. That is why she took Andy.

That day in 1931 was the first time the Great Depression affected my small world.

I became aware of other changes after Raggedy Andy went to live with Tommy. Some of my friends in the neighborhood had to go away and live with their grandparents because their parents couldn't afford to feed them.

Often, we would hear a knock on the back door, and there stood a homeless man asking if he could do some odd jobs in exchange for a meal. My mother would tell him to sit on the back steps while she fixed some food for him. I sat next to him and talked with him until Mom came out with a hot dinner. She never refused anyone who asked for food.

My brother needed a Boy Scout uniform, and our parents couldn't afford a new one. Word went out to friends and neighbors, and one evening, a man came over with a complete Boy Scout uniform that someone had outgrown. There was even a knapsack, canteen, boots and stockings. I can remember how happy my brother was and how the family rejoiced.

Neighbors came over often to borrow a half cup of sugar or "a little milk for my husband's coffee." Mom had to borrow things from neighbors too. They all gave to each other when they could. Everyone was in the same situation. When they had an abundance of anything, they shared it. We all learned to be innovative and make do with what we had.

Raggedy Andy

CLEOPATRA AND THE GRAPES OF WRATH

As I grew older, I became more aware that money was scarce. I accepted this as fact and observed that money was scarce for every family in town. There was no such thing as "instant gratification" in the Depression years. I understood this very well because in 1933, at age eight, I asked for a bicycle for my birthday. I didn't get one so I asked for a bicycle for Christmas. Christmas came and there was no bicycle by the tree.

I had developed a mantra by my ninth birthday. I knew exactly what I wanted, "a twenty-six-inch blue and white Elgin bike with balloon tires, a basket on the handlebars and a light." My ninth birthday passed with no bike in sight. My mantra was included in my prayers at night. When wishing opportunities came up, such as splitting a turkey wishbone or finding a four leaf clover or the "first star I see tonight," I repeated my description starting with, "a twenty-six-inch blue and white Elgin..."

In November of 1934, my sister, Mildred, planned a magnificent surprise birthday party for my mother. Mildred was twenty-three years old and had a job as a secretary. All the aunts, uncles, cousins, neighbors and special friends were invited. The house was packed. There must have been one hundred people milling around, laughing and talking. My sister was very busy seeing that everyone was having a good time.

My cousin, Shirley, and I looked for something to do to amuse ourselves. The grown up conversations held no interest for us. I looked at the dining room table. It was decorated beautifully and Mom's best dishes were being set on the sideboard in preparation for a buffet. In the center of the table was a great tray of fruit. Polished apples gleamed in the candle light, and perfect rosy pears peeked out from artistically placed grapes. Suddenly, I had an idea.

"I know! Let's play Cleopatra!" "How do you play that?" Shirley asked. "I'll show you. Just follow me," and I picked up the fruit-laden tray and carried it to my parent's bedroom, thinking they won't need it for a while, and I'll return it when the buffet starts. Handing Shirley the grapes, I threw myself on the bed and declared that I was Cleopatra and Shirley was my slave. "All you have to do is wave that paper fan at me and drop grapes in my mouth, one at a time."

Shirley was a sweet girl, very acquiescent; and, because she was younger than me, it was easy to get her to follow my instructions. She dutifully dropped the grapes in my mouth and waved the fan while I, Cleopatra on her barge, enjoyed the luxury. This went on for quite a while until Shirley was tired of her role as slave. "When's it going to be *my* turn to be Cleopatra?"

I dismissed this request with an impatient wave of my hand. "Just keep feeding me the grapes. I'll tell you when it's your turn."

"But the grapes are almost gone."

"Well then," I ordered, "Give me one of those pears."

Eventually, Shirley had been compliant long enough. She dropped the fruit on the bed and went in search of my mother. " Alice won't let me have a turn to be Cleopatra!" My mother and Mildred came into the bedroom to see what Shirley was complaining about. Mildred took one look at the skeleton grape vine and the fruit all over the bed and gave me a look I will never forget. She turned and stomped out of the room and my mother shook her head at me as she gathered what was left of the centerpiece.

The next morning my mother told me, "Well, you've really done it this time! Your sister has been saving her money all year to buy you a bicycle for Christmas, but after your stunt last night you can just forget about it."

So, Christmas of 1934 came and went, and no bike was by the Christmas tree. I really didn't expect to see one. July 1935 came. I made the same wish as I blew out my birthday candles but my blue and white Elgin didn't materialize.

By Christmas of 1935, I had given up all hope of ever getting a bicycle. I descended the stairs on Christmas morning and there, in front of the Christmas tree, stood my twenty-six-inch blue and white Elgin bike with balloon tires, a basket on the handlebars and a light.. The Christmas lights reflected on the fenders. My mother and father, sister and brother were smiling at me, and I screamed and jumped with joy. My dreams, my prayers, my wishes had come true. I dressed quickly and took my bike out in the melting snow to show my friends. Such a long wait and such utter happiness!

The long wait for a bicycle was not in retribution for the Cleopatra debacle as I found out many years later. The money that had been saved for my bike was used for unexpected family needs and it took another year to save enough for my gift.

CREATIVE LIVING

There were wagons and scooters that could be bought in stores, but the best scooters were the ones we made ourselves. Each homemade scooter was different, but the basic design was the same. It started with a board, about six inches wide and about thirty inches long. The wheels from old roller skates were attached to each end of the board. A wooden orange crate was nailed to one end of the board. Empty tin cans became "headlights" on the orange crate. A wooden stick on top of the orange crate was a handle. Special treasures could be stored in the orange crate.

Homemade Scooter
Sketch by Deborah Worthen

My brother helped me make my scooter and taught me to oil the wheels so it would go faster. We had sidewalk races to see how far we could coast. The oiled wheels helped me to win some of those races.

When spring arrived and the lilacs were blooming, it was time for our family's yearly ritual. We all went downstairs to the basement to make our homemade root beer. The laundry tub was filled with hot, soapy water; and my brother, Gordon, washed all the bottles using a bottle brush. My sister, Mildred, rinsed the bottles and turned them upside down. Mom measured the ingredients that went into a large brown crock. We all took turns stirring the mixture with a long wooden spoon.

When everything was mixed to Mom's satisfaction, she put a funnel in the opening of a clean bottle, line it with cheesecloth, and ladle just the right amount of mixture into the bottle. Mildred handed the bottle to Dad who sat ready with a contraption called a "bottle capper." My job was to place a bottle cap on top of the bottle and get my hand out of the way while Dad pressed the handle of the bottle capper down.

Crock and Bottle Capper

We had an efficient assembly line, and soon we had sealed enough bottles to last the whole summer. After all the bottles were filled, we carried them up to the attic to "cure" for a few weeks. During those weeks, it wasn't unusual to hear a loud explosion any time of the day or night. The combination of sugar, yeast and heat in the attic contributed to an explosive atmosphere. We lost five or six bottles due to explosion, but the majority survived.

After the curing time, they were carried down to the cool basement. We always had cool bottles of root beer in our ice box and could help ourselves and serve it to our friends whenever we liked.

Summertime was special for the children and the adults. It was a time to gather together, play, laugh, and forget about money problems. Our house was built on a corner lot. We had a large screened front porch. Around dusk, most of the neighbors would go for walks and end up on our front porch for casual conversation. My mother would serve cookies and fruit juice or our homemade root beer. There would be laughter and light-hearted bantering. Sometimes, my sister would play the ukulele and everyone would sing the popular songs.

The dim corner street light was our only source of illumination besides a citronella candle that cast moving shadows on everyone. It was a magical atmosphere. When I was little, I was allowed to stay up and enjoy the evenings. I don't remember being sent to bed, so I probably fell asleep in my mother's arms or on one of the visitor's laps.

The older children played baseball on the street corner. There were drainage grates at each corner curb. They served as bases. There was little, if any, traffic on our street so there was no danger from automobiles. Sometimes, the children played kick-the-can until dark. When I got to be eight years old, I joined the baseball games on the corner.

House on corner of Delphia and Stewart

One of the favorite pastimes of the preschool children in the neighborhood was playing cowboys and Indians, cops and robbers, or soldiers and enemies. It didn't really matter which one we played. The actions were all the same.

Sticks became rifles accompanied by shot sounds coming from our mouths. Hiding behind trees or houses, we quickly jumped into view making our rifle sounds. Shouts of, "I got you. You have to fall down!" were answered with, "No, you didn't. You missed me."

One day, while we were playing, a nice young lady came out of her house and gave each of the girls a nurse cap that she had made. Each cap had a red cross on the center front.

She informed us that girls are not soldiers; they are nurses. Girls help the wounded soldiers to heal.

Nurses
Sketch by Jean Grimm

We were impressed that this lady cared enough about us to reveal what our proper roles were. We were also proud to wear the nurse hats. The following day, the girls picked up the wounded soldiers and dumped them into wagons. The wagons were pulled to a "hospital" a few yards away. Not knowing exactly what nurses do to heal wounded soldiers, we waved our hands over them and said, "Okay, you're all better." And the boys returned to their regiments and resumed fighting their war.

This lasted a few days until we became bored with being nurses and longed to return to the dangers of the battlefield. It was much more fun to hide, run, and give lively performances of being shot than it was to cure soldiers. We chose another location for our battleground so the kind lady wouldn't know we had switched identities, became soldiers, and went on the with the business of ridding the world of enemies.

Paper dolls provided hours of entertainment on a rainy day. There were paper doll books in the stores, but they cost money. We cut out models from the Sears catalog and designed clothes on plain paper, coloring them with crayons.

Paper Dolls **Paper Dolls Dressed**

In July, the hollyhocks were in bloom. We made hollyhock dolls and floated them in a bowl of water. We had quite a few hollyhock plants that grew on the south side of our house. Some were red, some white and some pink. My favorites were the pink ones.

To make a hollyhock doll, pick one flower and one bud. Leave about ½ inch stem on the flower. Do not leave a stem on the bud. Peel off the green covering of the bud until you get to the white part. You will see several small holes at the base (stem end). Insert the flower stem into one of those holes. Float the dolls in a bowl of water. This makes a pretty centerpiece.

Hollyhocks

Flower **Bud** **Peel Bud**

Hollyhock Doll

Hollyhock Doll Instructions

Dolls in Bowl

There was no limit to the creative activities people designed. It didn't cost a cent to provide hours of fun and entertainment.

AUNT MARTHA AND THE EDGERTON GHOST

I was fortunate to have six loving aunts from my mother's side of the family, but I also had many unofficial aunts and uncles. My mother and father had close friendships with our many neighbors, and I called them all "aunts" and "uncles." To me, they were authentic loving relatives.

In addition to the real aunts and the neighborhood aunts, there were many of my mother's close friends from her "old neighborhood" in Chicago. One of them was Aunt Martha.

Aunt Martha had a granddaughter who was my age. Her name was Darlene. The Depression didn't seem to affect Aunt Martha's family. Darlene had all the toys and clothes a girl could want. I was not fond of Darlene. She was bossy and always had to have her way.

One summer, Aunt Martha invited my mother and me and my Aunt Mabel and cousin Shirley to her summer home at a lake near Edgerton, Wisconsin.

While Aunt Martha was driving, Darlene told Shirley and me about a beautiful young woman who had disappeared from the town of Edgerton. Nobody ever knew what happened to her.

As we neared the summer house, we passed a forest. Then Darlene expanded her story and, in loud whispers, she said, "Every night that woman's ghost comes out of the woods and roams around looking through the windows of the houses. People have seen her."

Shirley and I trembled as we got out of the car. The dense woods were very close to the back of the house. That afternoon, as we were wading in the lake, Shirley and I moved away from Darlene and I whispered, "Do you believe what Darlene said about the ghost?" Shirley shrugged her shoulders with an "I don't know" gesture. I said, "Well, I don't believe it. I think she made it all up!" Shirley said, "Me, too." Although we still weren't sure it was a fabricated story, just saying we didn't believe it made us feel safer.

Shirley and I slept together in a double bed that night. Something woke me from a sound sleep. I looked around the room and saw the window was wide open and the sheer curtains were waving furiously. I turned my head and saw a figure floating toward me. She had a white filmy gown that billowed around her and wild-looking white hair. *The Ghost!* My heart pounded as she came nearer. When she reached toward me I made a decision that I wasn't going to leave this world quietly. I sat up and screamed as loud as I could. Shirley bounced up next to me. I heard people running in the hallway and into our room as my screams continued. Someone turned on a light and Aunt Martha, standing in her white nightgown, was saying, "Alice! Alice! It's all right, dear. I just came in to cover you up and shut the window. There's a storm coming."

Ghost

THE RED RIBBON

The same summer as the "Edgerton Ghost," Aunt Martha persuaded my mother to let me go away to a YMCA camp for a week. I think Aunt Martha wanted her granddaughter, Darlene, to have someone with her that she knew. I had never been away from home before and I was surprised that my mother could afford to send me to camp.

I looked forward to the adventure, but I hoped Darlene and I wouldn't be in the same cabin. Unfortunately, when we arrived at camp and received our cabin assignments, Darlene and I shared a cabin along with six other girls. "Oh well," I thought, "I can have fun with the other girls in the cabin."

We had a counselor who was in charge of the eight of us. She told us the rules, introduced us to each other and asked us to tell something about ourselves. She was going to sleep in the cabin with us.

The first night (Sunday), we had a bonfire after supper and sang songs, told jokes, and made up ghost stories. I decided it was going to be a fun week. The next morning after breakfast, we were told to get into our swim suits. I searched my suitcase and couldn't find my swim suit. I asked the other girls if they had seen it and they giggled.

Darlene giggled the loudest. I continued looking until one of the girls suggested I look outside.

While the rest of the girls ran down to the lake, I started searching outside the cabin. I saw a blue scrap of material on the ground. I bent to pick it up but it was stuffed into a gopher hole. When I pulled it out, my new swim suit was covered with dirt. I found out later that Darlene had done it.

After washing my swimsuit and struggling into it while it was wet, I was late getting down to the lake where they were testing everyone on their swimming skills. The counselor decided I couldn't swim well enough to go in the deep water so they tied a red ribbon on my shoulder strap. That meant I had to stay within a roped-in shallow area.

After lunch, it was rest time. It was mandatory that we write a letter to our parents every day. That first day I was unhappy about Darlene and the rest of the girls. I also had my first experience of being homesick. I wrote to my mother and begged her to come and take me home.

The next day, we went horseback riding, which I thoroughly enjoyed. All the girls in our cabin, except Darlene, told me they were sorry and wanted to be friends. In a much happier mood during rest time that day, I wrote a letter to my family. I decided to tell them about the red ribbon, but I embellished the story so they would think I had been awarded the ribbon because of my expertise in swimming. I wrote, "I got a red ribbon on my bathing suit and that means I can swim pretty good." My mother kept that letter. I found it many years later after she had passed away.

The week went fast. I learned how to shoot at targets with a rifle. We made beautiful things in craft class, and I had made good friends.

When my parents came to get me on Saturday they were taken on a tour around the camp. They saw our crafts on display, the rifle range, tennis court, stables and the lake

When we got to the lake, my mother asked the counselor what a red ribbon meant. The counselor said, "Oh, that means she has to stay in the roped-in area because she can't swim."

My face turned red with embarrassment. I had broken two of my mother's laws:

(1) never lie and (2) don't boast. I was caught red-handed!

Mom didn't say a word. She didn't even give me "the look." I think she knew I would remember this lesson.

DIVERSIONS

While we children played, cheerfully unaware that the nation was sinking into hopeless desperation, our parents somehow managed to keep their fears from touching us. We had no knowledge of the "good life" of the past. Innocent and ignorant of any other lifestyle, we went about the business of play, making friends, and being happy.

One of my older cousins went away to a CCC camp after he graduated from high school. He worked with a construction crew that was building new roads. He had to live in a camp away from home. CCC was the abbreviation for Civilian Conservation Corps.

"Principal benefits of an individual's enrollment in the CCC included improved physical condition, heightened morale, and increased employability. Of their pay of $30.00 a month, $25.00 went to their parents."
From Wikipedia, the free encyclopedia

Bread lines and soup kitchens were forming in the big cities. There was an increase in the number of hungry men knocking on doors in our town, looking for handouts. They were never turned away empty-handed.

In 1934, as the nation sank deeper into dark despair, a curly headed little girl appeared on the movie screen to sing and dance into our hearts. For the small price of a movie ticket, Shirley Temple, with her dimpled smiles, brightened the spirits of men, women and children. My cousin and I read everything that was written about her, her family, her pets, and her pony. We collected pictures of her. We learned every word of her song "On the Good Ship Lollipop," and entertained our aunts and uncles at family gatherings with our rendition of the song.

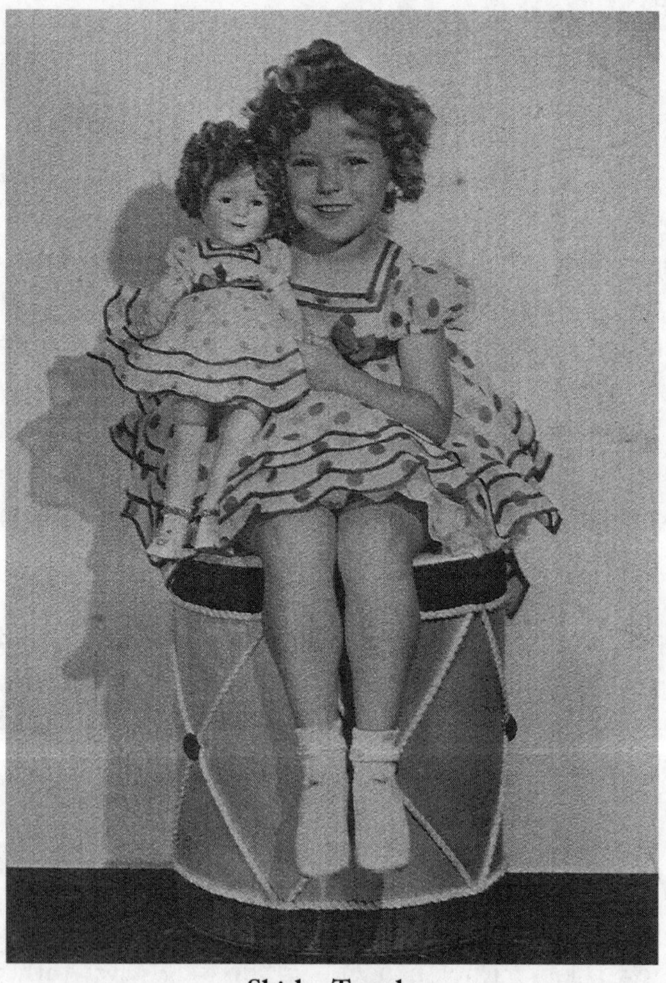

Shirley Temple

Shirley Temple Dolls
From Carol Licastro's Collection

Shirley Temple had dimples that appeared in her cheeks everytime she smiled. My cousin, Shirley, and I tried to see how we would look with dimples. We clamped the tissue of our inner cheeks between our molars and tried to smile to see if we could have dimples like Shirley Temple. We must have looked ridiculous.

Shirley Temple dolls appeared in the stores. Every little girl wanted one. Soon, Shirley Temple dresses were in the department stores. The average cost of a girl's dress at that time was $1.98, and very few girls had more than three dresses. Shirley Temple dresses sold for $2.98. In January, I asked my mother if I could have a Shirley Temple dress. She told me they were too expensive and I knew it would be useless to plead.

Six months later, on my birthday, I opened a box and took out a blue and white Shirley Temple dress like the one she wore in "The Littlest

Rebel." I think my sister helped pay for that dress. Two months later, cousin Shirley received a Shirley Temple dress on her birthday.

Littlest Rebel Dress

About the same time that Shirley Temple captured America's hearts, Canada had an occurrence that caught the attention of the entire world. The Dionne quintuplets were born in a farmhouse in Ontario, Canada. They were the first quintuplets to survive and thrive.

Pictures of the babies appeared in the newspapers and magazines. A movie was made about the birth of the "quints." Everyone followed the progress of those little girls: the first tooth and the first steps. They belonged to everyone, and everyone had a favorite. Mine was Marie, for no particular reason other than my middle name is Marie.

The world revolved around five adorable identical little girls. The Canadian government and the girls' parents took advantage of the adoring public and made great profit by showing them off.

The government took custody of the quintuplets and built a compound where the girls lived until they were nine years old. There were observation areas near the outdoor playground where, for a fee, the public could watch the girls at play. Thousands of people visited the compound every day.

The parents opened a souvenir shop nearby and cashed in on the public's curiosity, selling postcards, dolls, and photographs.

As we enjoyed more Shirley Temple movies and watched the quintuplets become toddlers, another diversion came from Great Britain. King George died in 1936; and his son, Edward, inherited the throne. He abdicated in order to marry Wally Simpson, a divorced American. His brother took the throne and he had two young daughters, Elizabeth and Margaret.

Elizabeth was my age. I read everything I could about the two princesses and collected pictures of them. I wondered how they felt, now that they were princesses. They had not expected to be princesses and, suddenly, their father was king, and they were living in a palace. Not only that, but Elizabeth would someday be queen. To me, it was like a fairy tale.

Princess Elizabeth
Painting by Phillip de Làszlò
This picture was taken from Wikipedia.

The people welcomed these diversions. For a little while, they forgot their worries as they read about the princesses and the quintuplets or watched Shirley Temple smile and dance. Those children and their own children were the hope of the future.

My girl friends and I were in awe of Amelia Earhart, an aviatrix who looked like a tomboy with short tousled hair and a boyish way of dressing. She was setting records for female pilots, and we twelve-year-olds admired her. She was in the newsreels at the movies many times. The last time we saw her, she was waving goodbye and getting into a plane to fly around the world. She was last heard from during that flight in July 1937 as she flew over the Pacific ocean. She never returned home, and there were no clues or wreckage to indicate what happened. We were heartbroken and hoped she had landed on a remote island. The world waited. Search parties went out to islands in the Pacific but they didn't find any answers. Seventy-five years later, at the time of this writing, there is renewed interest in her fate and divers are looking for wreckage.

Amelia Earhart
This picture was taken from Wikipedia.

Some songs of the 1930s reflected everyone's hope for better days. Their spirits brightened when they heard lyrics of such popular songs as:

1. "Happy Days Are Here Again." Lyrics by Jack Yellen. Music by Milton Ager. Franklin Roosevelt's campaign song in 1932

2. "Pick Yourself Up." Lyrics by Dorothy Fields. Music by Jerome Kern. From the movie, "Swing Time," 1936.

COUSIN SHIRLEY

My cousin, Shirley, and I were best friends for life. We grew up in a loving, close-knit family. My mother had six sisters and two brothers. When they all got together with their spouses and children at our house, there were more than thirty men, women and children scattered throughout the house. I had seventeen cousins, most of whom were older than me. Shirley and I were the two youngest.

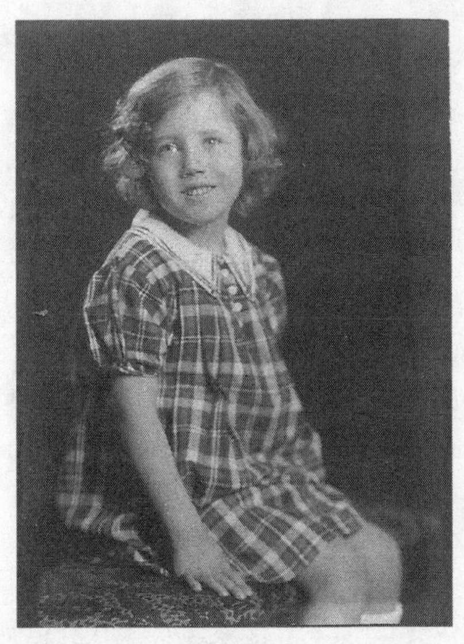

Shirley

I can remember only one time when we quarreled, and that was when we were very young. I was staying at Shirley's house for a few days and we were in her bedroom playing with paper dolls when we got into an argument. It progressed into name-calling and some pushing and shoving. Shirley grew so angry she grabbed a paper doll she thought was mine and ripped it in half. "So there!" she said with great satisfaction.

I stared at her in disbelief. Toys, even paper dolls, were precious commodities. We wouldn't think of destroying them. When I realized the doll was Shirley's, I laughed and gleefully informed her that she tore her own doll.

Enraged, she stomped out of the room to find her mother (Aunt Mabel). With tears flowing, she told her mother the things I had said and done, omitting her own part in the argument. Aunt Mabel listened, then said, "Well, if Alice keeps saying and doing those things she won't go to heaven."

Shirley let out a wail. "Now what?" Aunt Mabel asked. Between sobs, Shirley said, "I want Alice to go to heaven!" "Oh, for goodness sakes. Go back to your room and play nice." Aunt Mabel turned and walked away. When Shirley had calmed down, she came back to the bedroom to find that her broken doll had been mended with adhesive tape I found in the medicine cabinet.

Despite Aunt Mabel's grim prediction of my eternal future, I loved her very much. She was a funny lady—always cheerful, singing and telling stories. During school vacations, I would spend a week or two at Shirley's house. I was just as comfortable there as I was in my own home.

Aunt Mabel made a fantastic breakfast. She gave us toast with peanut butter and jelly on it. For our beverage, we had *coffee!*Actually, it was half milk and half coffee, and I loved it. I never had a breakfast like that at home. We had eggs or cooked cereal or pancakes at home. Never was I allowed a sip of coffee. Mom said it would stunt my growth. That didn't make sense to me because Shirley was two years younger than me and she was already taller than me.

Every little girl wanted to have a head full of curls like Shirley Temple. When we were getting ready to go to a family gathering, I would ask my mother if Shirley was going to have curls. Mom would call Aunt Mabel and, if the answer was "yes," I'd ask Mom to curl my hair.

My Aunt Mabel was good at rolling Shirley's hair in curlers to get the Shirley Temple look. My mother didn't have that talent. She used a curling iron on my hair. In those days, there were no electric curling irons. The curling iron was heated over a gas range. After a few minutes in the flames, it was tested by clamping the roller between a piece of paper. If the paper turned brown, it was ready, according to my mother.

Mom would clamp some strands of my straight hair and roll the curling iron close to my head. I still remember the smell of burning hair. When she finished curling all of my hair, I ran to the mirror to see the results. I had a head full of singed hair sticking out in all directions. Some of the hair was actually missing. And I smelled bad.

When we arrived at the family gathering, there was beautiful Shirley with shining, bouncing curls. There I stood. I looked like I had stuck my finger in a lamp socket and got electrocuted!

Sweet-faced, with a sweet disposition, always obedient, Shirley was an adorable little girl. As the baby of the entire extended family, Shirley was regarded by everyone, including me, as a little darling.

As for me, a tomboy, daredevil, with permanently skinned up knees; I could find trouble without even looking for it. I did have one ally in Aunt Lizzy. She told me I reminded her of herself when she was a little girl. "Full of the dickens," she would say as she hugged me.

Shirley spent many weekends and vacations at our house throughout our childhood and teen years. There was something about Shirley's placid nature that challenged me. One time, I wanted to show her a trick I had been practicing. I was about nine years old at the time. Up in my bedroom on the second floor, I sat on my window sill and told Shirley, "Watch this!" Then, hanging by my knees, I thrust my body backwards, head down, hands free.

Shirley screamed and ran downstairs to find my mother. I could hear her crying as I waited, still hanging, for her to come back. My mother called from the foot of the stairs, "Alice, stop frightening Shirley. Whatever you're doing, stop it now!" I pulled myself back into the bedroom, wishing Shirley had admired my trick instead of telling on me.

We had a perfect stage in our living room. There was a ten-foot archway in front of the steps that led upstairs. On a pole in this archway hung a heavy velvet drape. The purpose of the drape when it was closed was to keep the hot air from going upstairs during the winter.

Shirley and I used this curtain for the many skits and plays that we produced for our aunts and uncles. The piano was nearby, and I accompanied Shirley when she sang songs. We could open and close the curtain to change costumes between acts. I don't remember our relatives being impressed with our entertainment. They continued talking to each other while we presented our acts. But when we took our bows, a few of them noticed us and clapped politely.

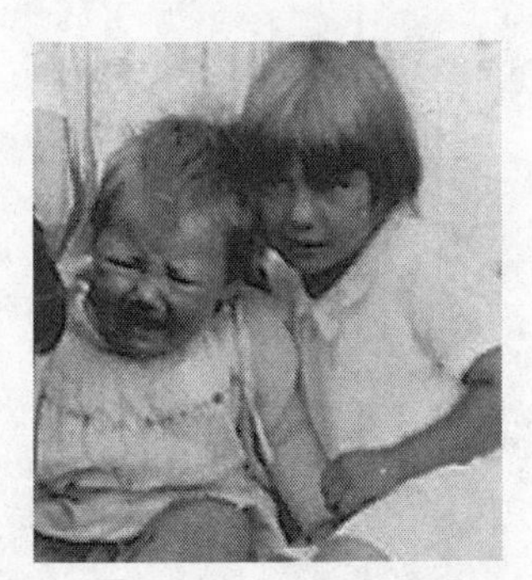

Shirley (crying) and Alice

Shirley and Alice

Shirley and Alice

Alice and Shirley wearing Shirley Temple dresses

As we grew older, we were allowed to ride the buses to movie theaters or other activities in Chicago. One time, we escaped the boredom of a long bus ride by pretending to be skaters in the Ice Follies. Sitting in the back of the bus, we held a long conversation with each other about our rehearsals and costume fittings and our close association with the stars of the show. When we reached our destination, our fellow passengers turned to see two giggling preteen girls exiting the back door of the bus.

As teenagers, we shared secrets and dreams of our future. We remained close friends throughout our lives.

Shirley and Alice

Alice and Shirley

When I married in 1947, she was my maid of honor. I moved to New Hampshire. Shirley married a few years later and moved to California. We couldn't be farther apart. However, we kept in touch with each other by letters and we did see each other several times. She was my first child's godmother.

The last time we saw each other was in 1996. We were both grandmothers and I was soon to be a great-grandmother. But when we were together, sitting at a table outside the Creamery with our husbands, eating ice cream cones, we were teenagers again—laughing and telling funny stories.

In the 1990s, phone rates had changed and long distance calls were no longer prohibitive, so we kept in touch by phone. I always enjoyed Shirley's subtle humor and her soft chuckle as she told me a joke or talked about an experience she had.

Time and distance do not diminish our vivid memories and our love for each other. As close as any sister, closer than a best friend, Shirley remains in my heart forever.

CLOTHING CASUALTIES

Clothes and shoes were low on the list of necessities in the Depression days. The primary concern was having enough money for food to eat and coal to heat their homes in winter. Clothes were not replaced unless it was absolutely necessary. Shoes were worn until they could no longer be resoled.

When shirt collars and cuffs became worn and frayed, they were detached, turned so the frayed side was not visible, and sewn back on. This gave the shirt a longer life and saved money for more important expenses.

Parents often bought their growing children a size larger than they needed and took deep hems in the dresses and trousers so the hems could be let down as the children grew taller. You could often tell when a hem had been let down on a dress because there was usually a trim of some sort sewn over the previous fold. One helpful hint to eliminate the telltale gray fold line of a lengthened skirt was to sponge the line with vinegar before ironing it.

One night, there was a knock at our back door, and there stood a man and his wife and thirteen-year-old son. They came into our kitchen and pointed to the son's ripped shirt. Mom called my brother to the kitchen and my father came also, to see what was going on. While I watched, the boy's father explained that his son and Gordon had got into a fight after school; and, as a result, his son's shirt was ruined. "What are you going to do about it?" he asked. They couldn't afford to buy a shirt.

My parents asked Gordon if this was true, and he admitted being in a fight with the boy. Mom went into her bedroom and came back with some money for the parents.

When I was in fourth grade, I wanted to tell something to the girl who sat in front of me. To get her attention, I reached out to pat her on the back, but, at the same time, she leaned forward and stood up. My hand landed on her belt and the belt broke in my hand.

That night, the girl's mother came to our house with the broken belt. It was an imitation leather belt. It looked like it was made of compressed cardboard. My mother compensated the girl's mother with no hesitation.

Many women made their own clothes and clothes for their children. Sometimes, an adult's worn-out coat could be cut and altered to fit a young person. Style was not particularly important during those hard times.

SATURDAY AT THE MOVIES

A RITUAL

The town I grew up in, Park Ridge, was a quiet little town. When my father bought our house in 1921, the population was only 3,383. "Downtown" consisted of two streets. Main Street ran parallel to the railroad tracks. Main Street had a bakery that always smelled of warm bread, cinnamon, and vanilla, and a butcher shop that had sawdust all over the floor. It was always fun to run and slide on the sawdust while my mother told the butcher what kind of meat she wanted and how she wanted it cut. There was also a grocery store. The owner stood behind a counter and my mother gave him her list. He went around to the shelves and gathered the groceries. There were no supermarkets at that time. The sugar and flour were in big barrels and if you wanted sugar or flour, the grocer filled paper bags and weighed them on a hanging scale. Housewives kept a careful watch to make sure the scale measured exactly what they ordered.

The other street was Prospect Avenue ,and it intersected Main Street. The business section of Prospect Avenue was only one block long, but it had all the stores I loved to spend time in. There was a drug store at each end of the block. Each drug store had a large soda fountain with a counter that ran the whole length of the store and red stools you could sit on and spin around. They served ice cream sodas, banana splits, hot fudge sundaes, and root beer, ginger ale and coca cola that came from special faucets. If I was lucky and had five cents, I could get an ice cream cone. Sometimes, when my Aunt Sadie came to visit, she would put a nickel in my hand when she kissed me goodbye and say, "Go buy yourself an ice cream cone," which is exactly what I did.

Prospect Avenue

In between the two drug stores were various stores, including Woolworth's five-and-ten-cent store—a magical place to spend time. There was also a bookstore and Robinson's, a combination of a candy store and an ice cream parlor.

But the most impressive building on the street was a beautiful modern-looking movie theater called the Pickwick. It still stands there today, just as elegant as ever, towering above the other buildings.

Pickwick Theatre

Saturday afternoons were made for the children of Park Ridge. From the age of eight on up, children left their houses at one o'clock every Saturday, walked to town and converged at the Pickwick for the matinee. I lived exactly one mile from downtown, and as I walked, girl friends joined me until there were four or five of us eagerly anticipating the afternoon's entertainment. The walk downtown was always a delight. The streets were lined with trees on each side that formed a green canopy overhead as far as you could see.

A Walk to Town

Our first stop was the candy store, right next door to the theater. I had fifteen cents in my hand. The movie cost ten cents, and five cents was for candy. We spent a great deal of time choosing our penny candy. We wanted to get the most value for our money. Most of the candies were in large bins behind a glass counter. You could get two licorice sticks for a penny or five bull's eyes for a penny. There were also peppermints, jelly beans, gum drops, and hollow caramel-flavored sticks. Lollipops, bubble gum and bags of popcorn were on display on the counter tops.

The clerk had exceptional patience with us. Every time I selected something and he reached for it, I'd say, "No—wait." After everyone had made their choices, we left the candy store armed with paper bags bulging with our favorite candies. We paid our ten cents at the ticket window and were ushered down the aisle to our seats. The usher wore a uniform and carried a flashlight. He always asked if we wanted to sit in the front, middle, or back of the theater. We asked for "middle-front."

The usher was in charge of everyone's deportment during the movie. If anyone was making noise, throwing paper gum wrappers or popcorn at others, or causing a disturbance, the usher came down the aisle, turned his flashlight on the culprit, and warned him to stop. If it continued, the guilty person was taken outside and was not allowed back.

The matinee started with six cartoons. Popeye, Mickey Mouse, Porky Pig were favorites.

Then there was a serial. This was a story that continued every week, picking up where it stopped the week before. It was always a lively adventure and we cheered and "booed" as we became absorbed in the plot. There was always a handsome daring hero, a beautiful maiden who needed to be rescued from a disaster, and a villain who plotted horrible things. Just as the maiden was dangling from a cliff, or being charged by a lion, the story would end, promising to return next wee k. I suppose this was how the expression "cliff-hanger" began.

After the serial came the travelogue. As soon as the opening music for the travelogue started, there was a great group moan which filled the theatre. The travelogue consisted of pictures of a foreign country narrated by someone in a monotone to an audience that had no interest in the subject. This was when most of the popcorn-throwing, fights, and loud talking occurred. Then the usher came down the aisle with his flashlight and several boys were led outside—never to return for the main movie feature.

When the travelogue ended, there was loud cheering and clapping, celebrating the end of boredom and the anticipation of the feature movie. When the feature film came on, we all sat quietly, absorbed in the plot, adoring the movie stars. When the movie was finished, you could leave and go home or, if it was a great movie, you could stay and see it all again free. It was a good idea to have prior approval from your parents. You could actually stay in the theater as long as you wanted and watch the movie over and over without paying any more money. I once stayed for three showings of Ginger Rogers and Fred Astaire in "Swing Time." It was a particularly fine movie with music and dancing. My mother was not pleased with me when I got home after six o'clock.

That was a typical Saturday afternoon in Park Ridge; one that I never missed, except for one Saturday in February when I was ten years old. I started out the door with my fifteen cents but turned back and told my mother I didn't feel well. This was so unusual my mother put me in bed and called the doctor. He came to the house, examined me, and announced that I had scarlet fever, a dreaded contagious disease; and the house was quarantined for six weeks. The Public Health people put a big red sign on our front door telling people to stay out.

I missed six weeks of school. The fifth grade class wrote "get well" notes one day and a boy was assigned to deliver them after school. I watched him from my bedroom window. He stood across the street and looked at our house for a long time. Finally, after taking a deep breath, he pinched his nose between his fingers and ran up the porch steps, dropped the notes on the porch, rang the doorbell and ran. He looked like he was going to pass out by the time he reached the other side of the street, lifted his head and took another breath.

Long division and multiplication were taught during the time I was absent and I still have trouble multiplying anything over the five times table. But missing school was not the worst consequence of being confined. I never found out what happened to the helpless maiden who was hanging on a cliff!

YOU'RE DARN TOOTIN'

One Saturday afternoon when I was about eight years old, I saw a cowboy movie. I was impressed with a cowboy who used a phrase I had never heard before. Another cowboy asked him a question and, instead of answering, "Yes," he said, "You're darn tootin'."

All the way home from the movies, I repeated that phrase, trying to make it sound like the cowboy. "You're darn tootin'." "Yer dern tootin'." I thought it was neat and couldn't wait until I had the opportunity to use it.

The following Sunday afternoon, the occasion presented itself. I was invited to a birthday party for one of my girl friends. After the cake, ice cream, games and prizes, it was time to go home. I remembered my manners and went up to Janet's grandmother and said, "Thank you very much."

She smiled sweetly at me, bent down, patted my head and said, "Did you have a nice time, dear?" This was my opportunity! I puffed out my chest and, in my best cowboy voice, I declared, "Yer dern tootin' I did!"

Her expression turned to horror as she straightened up, drew a deep breath and said, “What a nasty thing to say! I’m going to call your mother.”

As I walked home, I wondered why that was nasty. A well-respected actor had said those words in a movie theater. They must be all right. Well, which would it be? Loss of privileges? Sit on a stool in the kitchen? No movies next Saturday? I had no idea how serious this crime was.

When I arrived home, my mother said, “Mrs. Thompson called. What did you say to her?” I told her the dreaded words, “Yer dern tootin’,” and she was silent for what seemed like a long time. “She’s deciding my fate,” I thought. She seemed to have trouble controlling her mouth. Was that a smile she was trying to conceal?

I tried to justify my behavior. “A cowboy said that in a movie.” “Well, little girls don’t talk like cowboys to their elders. Just don’t say it anymore.” She turned to go into the kitchen. I waited to see if she would dole out punishment. Apparently, I was pardoned. As I heard the dishes rattle while she set the table for supper, I thought I heard a giggle.

THE AMATEUR HOUR

My oldest brother, Harold, was in college when I was born. By the time I was three years old, he was married. I don't remember a time when he lived at home. I regarded him more as an uncle than a brother.

Harold and Alyce, engaged

Alyce and Harold

When I was seven years old, Harold and his wife, Alyce (same name as mine except spelled with a Y), had a son. They named him Harold William. We all called him Billy. Two years later, they had another son. They named him Gene. I adored those two little boys and was proud to be their aunt. I was closer to them than I was to my brother, Harold.

Billy and Gene

In the mid-1930s, as a forerunner to "America's Got Talent," there was a popular radio program—The Major Bowes Amateur Hour. Major Bowes would interview a performer, ask questions about where he/she was from, etc.; and then it was time to show off his/her talent. The contestant either sang a song or played an instrument or did some tap dancing. There was no television at that time, so the show was based on sound. The listeners had to use their imaginations to visualize what the contestant looked like. If Major Bowes decided the performer was untalented, he hit a big gong right in the middle of the act. Then the listeners would either be sorry for the person or agree he deserved the gong.

During the hour, there were many contestants and the listeners had their favorites. Our family would pick our favorites, which might change if a better performer came on, and we waited anxiously to find out who the winner was at the program's end.

When my nephews, Billy and Gene, were pre-schoolers, I decided to become their manager and teach them how to tap dance in preparation for performing on the Major Bowes Amateur Hour.

Then, if they won on the amateur hour, they would have fame and fortune and everyone would be rich.

I took them downstairs to the basement and showed them some tap dance steps. Five-year-old Billy took a defiant stance, crossed his arms and said, "I'm not doing that!"

"Come on, Billy. It's easy."

"I don't care. I'm *not* doing it!" and Billy ran off. Gene, three years old, smiled up at me and said, "Ill do it, Alice." So, Gene tried and we worked at it until I decided we would probably get the gong anyway. I looked for other ways to make money.

Billy at Annapolis Naval Academy

Gene and Alice, Still Dancing

CARNIVAL CATASTROPHE

Every summer a carnival came to our town. It set up in a large field near the community swimming pool, and it lasted a week. I looked forward to that week all during the year. The evening sky was almost dark when our family arrived for the festivities, and the lights were on all the rides; music filled the air from the carousel; and the aroma of hot dogs delighted our noses. It was a magical time and place. My father gave me money to buy tickets to the rides, and I ran off to find my girl friends.

About 9 p.m., when it was really dark, a special show started and everyone gathered for the event. The one I remember was the tightrope act. Outdoors, high in the air, with spot lights focused on them, men and women walked across a thin wire. Some jumped rope or did a hand stand. I watched with admiration. All the townspeople were quiet as the act continued. Then, a man dressed in white with sparkling sequins on his shirt mounted a bicycle and rode slowly across the wire, balancing himself with a pole he held. I was sure he would fall and I wanted to close my eyes but fascination kept me following him until he was safely on the other side.

When I was eleven years old, I decided to have a carnival in my own back yard. I made posters to advertise the coming event and fastened them to telephone poles and trees in the neighborhood. In preparation for the free side show, my girl friends and I made hula skirts by cutting colored tissue paper into thin strips. We choreographed a hula dance and practiced it until we were all doing the same dance moves together.

A carnival isn't a carnival without a ride, so I devised one and had to enlist the aid of my brother, Gordon. I asked him to attach springs to our wheelbarrow and attach a board to the other end of the springs. When the customer sat on the board, Gordon pushed the wheelbarrow around the yard, bouncing the rider up and down on the springs. Once around the yard cost a penny. This ride was very popular and many of the children wanted second and third rides. Gordon was getting tired but he continued to power the ride.

Carnival Ride
Sketch by Deborah Worthen

Our garage was the "Spook House." I covered all the windows so the inside of the garage was black. We had an old Victrola (a phonograph that played music records. It was made before electricity was invented). We had to wind it up with a crank to make the turntable go around. I played a record of Edvard Grieg's "Peer Gynt Suite—In the Hall of the Mountain King." That was the spookiest music I could find. People entered the side door of the garage and were ushered through makeshift hallways where spooks jumped out occasionally and said, "Boo!" There were paper skeletons and other surprises. At the end of the walk through the dark Spook House, there was a log on the floor. One of my helpers was stationed by this log and gave the customer a push as he/she stumbled on the log and landed on an old mattress. Judging from the screams coming from the garage, the Spook House was a great success. As soon as the customers exited the garage, they lined up to go in again.

Other attractions were games of chance. Ringtoss and bingo drew a crowd. Prizes were my old comic books and toys. One of the games was throwing a baseball at a pyramid of empty tin cans. I had a problem with this game. I had plenty of cans but I didn't have a baseball.

I asked my brother if I could borrow his baseball. He was eighteen years old and played on a team that had uniforms. He hesitated and I begged. Finally, he said, "Okay, but you be sure not to lose it!" I promised gleefully as he handed me his baseball.

This was where the catastrophe started. A boy who was my age paid a penny and threw the ball at the cans I had set up on a wooden box. They all came down and he chose one of the old comic books for his prize. He decided to try it again, so I set up the pyramid of cans and he knocked them all down. This went on until I ran out of comic books. I offered him a choice of the old toys that were left. He said, "I don't want any old baby toys. But I'll try it again for this baseball." I told him the baseball was not a prize, so he said, "Okay, then I won't waste a penny on any of those other old prizes."

I wanted that penny. As he walked away I said, "Wait! Okay, but this time you have to knock them all down and *off* the box." He agreed and I set up the cans, confident that he couldn't knock them clear off the box. He wound up and threw the ball with all his might… the cans came tumbling down. Every one of them fell to the ground. I stared in horror. He picked up the ball and said, "See ya!" and walked away.

What was I going to tell my brother? I was in big trouble. When the carnival ended and I picked up the remnants of the afternoon I walked up to Gordon with great fear and told him what happened to his baseball. I said I'd give him all the pennies I had from the carnival. This amounted to seventy-six cents. I told him I'd give him any money I got for my birthday which was coming in two weeks. He looked at me and said, "Naw, that's okay. Forget it."

Oh sweet forgiveness! An unexpected reprieve. From that moment on, my brother became my hero and we were close friends for life.

MY BROTHER, FRIEND AND FOE

My brother, Gordon, was seven years old when I was born. He was disappointed that I wasn't a boy. By the time I was old enough to tag along after him, he had his own friends and interests and couldn't be bothered with a pesky kid sister. However, there were times when he took delight in making me scream.

Mom occasionally asked him to vacuum the living room rug. If I happened to walk by him while he was vacuuming, he swiftly lifted the bottom of that Hoover upright vacuum to my face. All I saw was those roaring jaws ready to suck me into that black bag. I'd jump up on the sofa, which was a mistake because I was trapped, and he would hold that hungry creature up to me until I screamed. That vacuum cleaner was so loud my screams were drowned out by its roar. When Gordon was satisfied that I was terrified, he resumed vacuuming; and I escaped.

Gordon and Alice

The highlight of our day came at 5:45 p.m. when Mom left us alone to drive downtown and pick up Dad at the train station. She was gone only ten minutes. but during that time, Gordon and I took the opportunity to express our animosity toward each other. I would call him a name and he started chasing me all over the house. We always ended up at the dining room table where he chased me around and around. I warned him, "If you hit me I'll break all your model airplanes!" He responded with, "You do that and I'll smash all your dolls!" When it looked like he was catching up with me, I quickly darted under the table and out the other side.

The minute we heard the car pull into the driveway we both stopped running and settled into our "good little kids" mode. Mom and Dad came in the house and saw Gordon peacefully reading a book on the sofa and me on the floor coloring in my coloring book.

One time, when Mom left to pick up Dad, Gordon came up to

me and said, "Come here, I want to show you something." I was suspicious. This didn't seem like our customary battle cry. I followed him into the dining room and he pointed to the table.

"I just did that," he said. I looked, horrified, at a puddle of ink sitting on top of a neatly folded, freshly ironed stack of Mom's best tablecloths. There was an ink bottle next to it. I started to feel sorry for Gordon, but a sly smile started on my face. I knew my mother would be very unhappy with Gordon. "Oh, Oh… You're gonna get it!" I said. With that, my brother walked over to the table and picked up the ink spot which was made out of tin and said, "April Fool!"

I was a little disappointed, but when he put it back on the tablecloths I said, "You aren't going to show that to Mom, are you?" He puffed out his chest to prove how brave he was and said, "Of course!"

I had to see this. When Mom came home and saw the ink spot she just smiled and walked away. She must have guessed from my giggling that this was a trick. We didn't have the satisfaction of watching a dramatic reaction.

By the time I was nine or ten, Gordon and I called an unspoken truce. He didn't bother me and I didn't aggravate him. It was when I was eleven that I looked at him in an entirely different way, as I explained in my story about Carnivals.

In February 1935, Gordon caught scarlet fever from me. I recovered with no side effects, but Gordon developed serious complications. In those days, doctors made house calls. He came to our house every day. First, he stopped in my room, checked my temperature and listened to my heart. I'd ask him when I could get out of bed, and he would pat my head and say, "soon." I was already getting out of bed when nobody was watching. When the doctor was finished with me, he would go to Gordon's room. He spent a lot of time with him.

I remember the whole house had a peculiar smell during that time. I just thought that was what scarlet fever smelled like. When I grew up and came across that smell again, I found out it was Lysol. My mother had wiped everything with Lysol to disinfect the house. Our house was quarantined, which meant that nobody could come in. My sister had to move in with one of our aunts in Chicago and ride a street car to work instead of the train. My father was allowed to live at home and go to work.

One day, the doctor talked with my mother for a long time, Gordon's health had deteriorated drastically. He had lost a lot of weight and had no energy. The urinalysis tests were alarming. Mom phoned my father at his office. That was the first time I heard my mother cry. Gordon was in critical condition and the doctor recommended my parents send him to a warm, sunny climate as a last resort. He was sent to Los Angeles to stay with my father's sister.

We all waited and prayed for Gordon's recovery. Several months passed and there was no improvement. Two more months and we received a phone call. Gordon was gaining weight and improving rapidly. In June, we received a picture of him standing on a diving board at a swimming pool, no longer weak and thin. He had gained his weight back and developed muscles. Mom and Dad wanted him back, and we all rejoiced when he arrived in July.

Gordon in California

Family Reunited, July 1935

He had some stories to tell us. One, I remember, was that he was in downtown Los Angeles when he saw the actress, Bette Davis. She was in a scene from the movie, "Dangerous," and she had to walk down the steps in front of a building. She repeated the scene many times until the director was satisfied. Miss Davis noticed Gordon watching her and she walked over to him and asked his name and where he was from. They talked for a while and she was very nice to him. She gave him her autograph and shook hands with him.

After he graduated from high school, Gordon was lucky to find a job at a tool and dye establishment. The money he made, when added to Mildred's contributions, helped the family greatly.

When I was twelve years old, I wanted to take ballet lessons. Mom said there was no money for that, but Gordon graciously offered to pay for the lessons. I took lessons for two years and then decided I wanted to learn to play the violin instead. Gordon agreed to pay for the violin lessons, and this continued for several years because he became enamored with my cute teacher and started dating her.

During the years between 1937 and 1941, while Gordon was working, he and I developed a close friendship. The seven years between us didn't seem so great and the distance in our ages grew shorter as our interests merged. Gordon took flying lessons in 1941 and, on the days he decided to get some solo flying time in, he would pick me up at my high school after classes and take me along for the flights. He flew a small Piper Cub airplane, and I loved to look down and see the farms and towns from a different perspective.

Gordon Takes Flying Lessons

Gordon and one of his friends, Bob, built a twenty-five–foot. sailboat. They worked on it for almost three years. On Saturday mornings, I went to the empty lot where they were constructing the boat and climbed around, trying to be of help by handing them nails and various tools. When it was finished, they included me as part of the crew when they sailed in Lake Michigan.

Building Sailboat

Bob Working on Sailboat

Finished Boat

Gordon and Bob with Friends

On December 7, 1941, Sunday, my mother and father and I drove to the small airport to meet Gordon and Bob. They had been on a cross country flight for several days. While we were waiting, someone who parked near our car and had his radio on said, "Did you hear that? The Japanese bombed Pearl Harbor!" Thus began World War II, an era that changed all Americans' lives.

Gordon joined the Navy, and we only saw him once over the war years; but we wrote often. When the war ended, he went to the University of Illinois for four years. During that time, I got married and moved to New Hampshire. Gordon found his true love at age 34, and was married in Park Ridge. We attended the wedding. I had three children by then.

His love of sailing continued throughout his life. He always lived near Lake Michigan, and I spent several vacations riding in his sailboat and learning how to water ski.

Gordon in Navy Uniform

STEP BACK IN TIME

If you didn't live through the Depression, you will have a hard time imagining what life was like then.

First, visualize a world without computers, cell phones, television, digital cameras, microwave ovens, air conditioning, malls, fast food chains, contact lenses, GPS. This is just a partial list of the things that didn't exist.

Now, take a step back in time to see how life was in the years 1930–1939. Most homemakers stayed at home to raise their children, make the meals, and keep the house in order. It took all of her time to accomplish this without the modern conveniences we enjoy now.

Our perishable foods were kept cool in an ice box. The ice man delivered large chunks of ice which would last four or five days, depending on the weather temperature. As the ice melted, the ice water dripped into a pan underneath the ice box. The pan had to be emptied often. An ice box wasn't cold enough to keep ice cream frozen. If you were going to serve ice cream, you had to buy it at the store, bring it home and serve it immediately. In our town,

Scharringhausen's drug store delivered ice cream for birthday parties and other occasions.

Our telephones were on a "party line." There were three other families who shared the same line. If you picked up your phone to make a call and heard people talking, you had to hang up and wait until they were finished. If the line was clear when you picked up the receiver, you would hear someone say, "Operator. Number, please." Then you told her the number you were calling and she would connect you. There were no dial phones. The phone numbers were short. Our phone number was 565R. By the way, there were no answering machines either.

There were no supermarkets. There were grocery stores, butcher shops, bakeries, and drugstores. There was no self-service. You told the clerk or proprietor what you wanted, and he would go to the shelves and get the items for you, take your payment, and give you change. There were no aspirins, band-aids and cold medicines at grocery stores, and there were no groceries in drugstores.There were ice cream and soda fountains at drugstores.

Stores were never open on Sundays. Sunday was a day of rest. We went to church or Sunday school in the morning. Nobody did yard work, laundry, cleaning or any manual labor. As a child, I was not allowed to sew clothes for my dolls or wash my bike on Sundays. I wondered why my mother was immune from those rules. She always made Sunday dinner and supper and washed the dishes afterwards.

In those years, everyone was affected by the stock market crash. For our family, we struggled along on whatever jobs my father could find. On rare occasions, some wealthy person would commission my father to design and engrave a special piece of jewelry. That would tide us over for a while and might even give us a few luxuries. However, my father had to set some of the profit aside to purchase precious metals (e.i., gold and silver) for the next jewelry order.

We never went hungry. Our closets had just a few clothes but that didn't matter to us. When holes appeared in the soles of my shoes, I would find some cardboard and slip it inside my shoe. When the cardboard wore out, I found another piece of cardboard. It didn't embarrass me. Everyone had holes in their shoes.

On rare occasions, my mother would surprise us with a treat. After supper, while we were all in the living room listening to the radio, Mom would occasionally come into the room carrying a small dish of candy. It was a Baby Ruth candy bar cut in small slices. We each took a slice. We never had a whole candy bar for ourselves.

Other times, we would make popcorn. We put the kernels in a metal mesh basket with a long handle and took turns shaking it over the gas flame on the kitchen stove.

It may seem like life was harsh, but, the truth is, we were happy, loving, and appreciative of little things (like one-fifth of a Baby Ruth bar). In warm weather, we played outdoors with our friends from morning until the street lights came on. In cold weather, we played Monopoly, checkers, read books, sewed clothes for our dolls, and listened to the radio.

Family friends, aunts and uncles gathered at our house often, and the atmosphere was lively and cheerful. There was much laughter and story-telling. Included in these gatherings were seventeen cousins. The majority of the cousins were in their early teens. Shirley and I were the youngest. All the cousins were loving and fun to be with.

There may have been some restrictions on what we could do on Sundays, but riding in a rumble seat was a great way to spend a

Sunday afternoon; and Shirley and I spent many Sundays in our uncle's rumble seat with our hair blowing while he drove us around the countryside.

Today, we can do our laundry any hour of any day and be done in less than two hours. In the 1930s laundry took two days. The wash was done on Monday, and it took all day. A tub type washing machine was used. Then the clothes were put through a hand operated wringer, soaked in rinse water, then put through the wringer again. After the rinse, shirt collars and cuffs were soaked in starch to make them stiff. The same water was used for all the loads so there was an order for the loads:

> First load. shirts, sheets, towels, tablecloths, and all white things.
>
> Second load. light colored clothes
>
> Third load. dark clothes
>
> Last load. extremely dirty work clothes
>
> Then the wash was hung on clotheslines outdoors and brought in when dry.

Tuesday was ironing day. All clothes needed to be ironed. There were no "wash-and-wear" fabrics. It took most of the day to iron all the clothes. There were no steam irons, so the clothes were sprinkled lightly with water, rolled up to distribute the moisture evenly, then ironed and hung on hangers to dry completely.

The laundry was always done on those two days, and more often if there was a baby in the family as there were no disposable diapers.

Some customs that we took for granted during that period of time are no longer observed today. If you have ever watched old movies that were made in the 1930s and 1940s, I'm sure you have noticed that all men wore hats. The fedora was a popular hat that was worn in the fall, winter and spring. When the straw hats came out of the closets, you knew summer had arrived.

Tipping the hat was a sign of respect when a man approached a lady. There was a protocol for the degree of respect he wished to convey. A slight touching of the hat's brim indicated the man was acknowledging a lady (probably a stranger) as they passed each other on the street. Lifting the hat was a polite, silent way of saying, "How do you do?" to a lady who was an acquaintance. Lifting the hat and bowing from the waist was the ultimate show of respect for special people. The man made the first gesture of tipping his hat and then waited for the lady to speak. He didn't speak first. If the lady wanted to make conversation, she indicated it by speaking first.

A man always took his hat off when entering a building. He never kept it on when he was in church or in a restaurant. Some of the better restaurants and night clubs had a hat check room where hats were stored and the man was given a numbered ticket to retrieve it. A monetary tip was expected for this service.

Conversely, women wore hats and gloves indoors to almost every social gathering and always wore them in church. There were hats for all the seasons, but the prettiest ones were the Easter hats and the wide-brimmed summer hats.

Other customs that are seldom seen these days involve gentlemen opening the car door for ladies and walking on the street side of the sidewalk when escorting a lady. These customs may have originated before the automobile was invented. When people traveled in horse-drawn carriages, women needed help to climb into carriages because the step was high and their long skirts hindered them.

When they went for walks, the man placed himself on the street side of the sidewalk to protect the woman from runaway horses and mud that sprayed from carriages passing by.

The customs have disappeared and some of the essence of those days have disappeared along with them.

I FELL IN LOVE WITH MY SISTER'S BOYFRIEND

My sister, Mildred, always wanted a sister. Unfortunately, fourteen years passed before I was born so I wasn't in time to be her pal or confidante. However, she included me in her social life from the beginning.

When Mildred and her girl friends went to the beach, they took me along. When they gathered on the front porch to play the ukulele and sing songs, I was right there, sitting on their laps, singing with them. Even when boys were invited to Mildred's parties and they danced to phonograph records in the living room, I was allowed to sit in the stairway to watch until it was time for bed.

Mildred, left, Alice, and two of Mildred's Friends

Mildred and Alice

Beach Party. Mildred and Friends and Alice

Mildred and Friend Wearing Beach Pajamas, Forerunner of Ladies' Slacks

Alice in Beach Pajamas, 1930

Mildred went to work as a secretary after graduating from high school. The Depression had just begun and the difficult years would continue for almost a decade. Mildred gave most of her earnings to Mom and Dad, keeping out just enough for incidentals and train fare to and from work. Years later, my mother told me there were times when Mildred's salary was the only money the family had to live on.

I loved to wake early in the mornings and climb into Mildred's bed to watch her get ready for work. She was a fastidious dresser. She always brushed her suit with a clothes brush before putting it on. Her shoes were shined the night before so they were ready. I would watch her put her make-up on and fix her hair. When she was finished, she held her hand mirror and turned her face from one side to the other with a critical look. Then, she would blot her lipstick and put a stray curl in place and she was ready to go. She was beautiful!

Beautiful Mildred

In the early 1930s, with the influence of musical movies, tap dancing became the rage. Mildred and her friends took tap dancing lessons in someone's basement and I was right there with them learning the time step and the "shuffle off to Buffalo." Ginger Rogers was my idol and I dreamed of some day dancing with Fred Astaire, wearing a flowing gown of white feathers.

In 1932, Mildred had a steady boy friend. He was tall, handsome and funny. His name was Ed. I adored him. When he came to take Mildred on a date, he always brought me a small gift: crayons, a coloring book, pencils, or a package of chewing gum. I looked forward to seeing him because he talked with me while he waited for Mildred to come into the living room. He made me feel special. A few times, they took me with them on their dates, and I rode in the "rumble seat" of Ed's car.

Mildred and Ed

I assumed Ed would always be a part of our lives when, suddenly, Ed stopped coming to the house. I asked Mildred why he didn't come anymore, but she didn't give me an answer. I kept waiting for him but he never came back. My heart was broken. I missed him so much.

Several years went by and Mildred had other boyfriends, but none of them measured up to Ed. Five years passed. Mildred had been dating a man named Bill for two years. One night she came home from a date with Bill and, instead of going to her bedroom, she came upstairs, climbed in bed with me, snuggled up and whispered, "Alice, how would you like to have another brother?" I sat up and asked, "Is Mom going to have a baby?" Mildred laughed and said, "No, I mean how would you like it if I married Bill? He would be your brother-in-law."

This was Mildred's first chance to share a secret with her sister. I was twelve years old and she was bursting to tell the good news. What was my answer to her sweet confidence?

"But what about Ed!" I was still carrying the torch. How could Mildred consider marrying anyone else?

"Alice, forget about Ed. Bill and I are going to be married. You are going to be my maid of honor." This was something to contemplate.

"Really?"

She nodded.

"Will I have a long dress?"

"Yes, and it will be blue."

"And can I carry a bouquet of pink roses?"

"If you want."

She was glowing with happiness. It was our first sister-secret. I hugged her and told her I was happy for her. We cuddled and she told me more wedding plans until I fell asleep.

Mildred and Bill were married a year later and they had three children. I was sixteen when their first child, Charles (Chuck), was born. After I was married and had children, we finally became the true confidantes and best friends we were destined to be. We spent many years visiting each other in Chicago and Pennsylvania, going on trips together, and talking on the phone in the late evenings when the rates were lower. A fourteen year difference in age is not such a wide chasm when you are in your fifties and sixties.

Inevitably, the time came when both of us had gray hair. Since we had a strong resemblance to each other, strangers would ask if we were sisters. We would say we were. Mildred always loved it if they asked, "Which one is the oldest?"

Even in our old age, I couldn't get an answer from Mildred whenever I asked, "But, whatever happened to Ed?"

Mildred and Alice

WHAT PRICE BEAUTY?

A PERM IN THE 1930s

There was a formal engagement several months after Mildred told me her secret. Bill asked our father for his daughter's hand in marriage. After receiving approval, Bill came to our house to formally propose to Mildred. The whole family went to the kitchen so the couple could be alone. It took a long time and I was restless.

"Can't I go in there and find out what's taking them so long?" I asked.

My mother told me to be patient. At last, the happy couple appeared and Mildred showed off her engagement ring. It was no surprise because my father had designed and made the ring. The engagement lasted ten months. I had turned thirteen before they were married.

Mildred had definite ideas of what kind of wedding dress she wanted, and she designed her own dress. She favored a tailored style, and, I must say, it suited her perfectly. With tiny, cloth covered buttons all the way up her back to her neck and a fitted bodice, her figure was displayed to full glory.

On the other hand, a fitted dress on my thirteen-year-old figure was not in the least bit flattering. We must have made twenty trips to the dressmaker to stand still while she measured and pinned and cocked her head to one side, then pulled out the pins and started all over. To me, an active child, each fitting seemed like an eternity.

At last, the dresses were finished. The invitations had been sent. Wedding gifts were arriving and put on display. There was one thing left. I was to get my hair cut short and have a *permanent wave*! My hair was long and I wore it loose with a hair band to keep it back out of my eyes. In hot weather I braided it. That was the extent to which I fussed with my hair, except when I was in my Shirley Temple phase five years earlier.

I went to the beauty shop alone. The beautician had been given instructions by my sister. Early perms were painful and dangerous. Some people received serious burns and permanent damage to their scalps.

As I sat in the chair, large gobs of my hair fell to the floor while the beautician snipped. Then some disgusting smelly stuff was smeared on my hair. The odor was overwhelming. Ammonia! Strong enough to make me gasp.

I was placed under a machine that had long electric wires hanging down. At the end of each wire was a clamp. Strands of my hair were wound around a rod and then one of the clamps was attached to it. When all of my hair was attached to those dangling wires, I was left alone to hear my hair crackling with the heat and smell the ammonia as it sizzled under the clamps. The clamps were heavy and I felt like my neck was breaking. I had seen a movie that had a scene of an electric chair execution and I tried not to think about that. Instead, I wondered what would happen if fire broke out in the building and I was attached to this electric octopus.

Permanent Wave Machine
This picture is courtesy of Grayslake
Historical Society, Grayslake, Illinois

When the process was finished, my hair was dry, frizzy and breaking off when it was combed.

Frizzy Hair

Mildred was married at home with all the aunts, uncles, cousins, and family friends present. She came down the stairs and my father walked her to the fireplace where Bill and the Pastor were waiting. Toward the end of the service, I could hear my mother start to cry. Then, the reality set in. My sister and Bill would leave tonight for San Francisco where Bill would start his new job. All the way across the country! I might never see her again.

As soon as the ceremony was over and everyone was congratulating the couple, I hurried to Mildred's room, shut the door, sat on the bed and cried. In a few moments, the door opened. It was Mildred. "What's the matter, Alice?" I was not a weepy type and I couldn't explain why I was crying. I just shrugged. She put her arm around me. "We'll write to each other a lot," she assured me. I couldn't stop crying.

"Look," she pointed to her maple bureau. "You can have my bureau." My sobbing stopped suddenly. "I can?" She nodded and hugged me.

"And your dressing table with the mirror? Can I have that?"

"Yes, and you can have my desk and the bed. You can have the whole room!"

Mildred's maple furniture that she bought with the money she earned. And her room was on the first floor, right near the hall where the telephone was. And her closet door had a full-length mirror. And there were white venetian blinds on the windows! I wiped my eyes with the back of my hands and hugged her.

Mildred and Bill stayed in California for just two years. When she became pregnant with her first child, they moved back to the Chicago area to be near the people they loved. Eight years after Mildred's wedding, I wore her wedding dress at my own wedding and it fit me perfectly.

And perms have improved greatly since the 1930s.

Mildred as a Bride

Mildred

Maid of Honor

Mildred

Mildred and Bill with Chuck

HOLIDAYS

Our town went all out for Memorial Day. Memorial Day was called "Decoration Day" in the 1930s. That was because it was the day everyone decorated the graves with flowers to honor the deceased, especially the soldiers who had died in the wars.

There was always a parade that almost everyone participated in. It started in town and ended at the cemetery where the mayor made a speech. The mayor always led the parade in an open car, followed by former soldiers from World War I, who marched to the music of a community band.

Boy Scouts, Girl Scouts, and Camp Fire Girls marched to the high school marching band. The junior high school band played march music for children on bicycles and tricycles. Following them were little girls pushing doll carriages and little boys pulling wagons. The bicycles, doll carriages and wagons were all decorated beautifully and were judged at the end of the parade. Everyone, including me, put a great deal of work into their decorations, hoping to receive the prize—a blue ribbon—from the judges.

My aunt Tonie was good at decorating with crepe paper and tissue paper. She showed me how to make special paper flowers and ruffled streamers to weave in and out of the spokes of my bike. Every year, as I worked tirelessly at the task, my mother would say, "Now, don't expect to win. Not everyone can be a winner." And every year I would think, "Of course I expect to win. Why else would I be working this hard?"

I never won.

When I became a Camp Fire Girl, I left my bike home and joined the marchers. Our leader, Mrs. Fulde, started practicing us in April during the weekly meetings at her house. Down in her basement, she taught us "Right Dress," "Forward March," "About Face," "Halt, one two" and other commands. She was very particular about our marching and keeping in step. Our lines had to be perfectly straight. When she said, "Halt, one two" we took exactly two more steps and stopped, both feet together. No stragglers allowed. We practiced "Halt, one two" until it was perfect. She was more strict than a drill sergeant. As a result, bystanders applauded when we marched by in perfect formation.

I don't know why we had to learn "About Face." We never used that when we were in a parade. Maybe it was because when we reached the other end of her basement, we could turn around and continue marching.

Camp Fire Girl

A day we celebrated when I was a child has been dropped over the years. That was May Day. Children made paper baskets, put a flower or a drawing in them, and hung them on neighbors' doors early in the morning on May first. We enjoyed making the baskets out of colored paper, and loved to watch people discover them at their doors.

Halloween was different than it is now. There was no "trick or treat." We were allowed to go out at night and play tricks on people. The most common trick was waxing the windows of neighbors' houses and cars. My mother didn't allow me to use wax because it was too hard for people to remove. She gave me a piece of soap to use, which was fine with me.

My friends and I dressed in whatever costumes we could dig up and went through the neighborhood, soaping windows and ringing doorbells, then running to hide. The older boys did the nasty tricks like dumping out garbage cans and stringing toilet paper on trees.

It wasn't until my last childhood Halloween that "trick or treat" started in our town. I was thirteen. This was a new concept for the children and the adults. We weren't quite sure how to do it. My girl friend and I decided to give it a try.

We walked for several blocks, then stopped at a house and rang the doorbell. Tempted to run, we turned back to the sidewalk just as the door opened. Two old ladies stood there smiling. We said, "Trick or treat."

"What, dear?"

"Trick or treat."

"What does that mean, dear?"

"It means if you give us a treat, we won't soap your windows."

"Oh, well do come in, then." They held the door open wide and ushered us in. "Please, won't you sit down?" one of them said as she sat on a chair in the living room. The other lady said, "I'll be right back with a treat," and she disappeared.

Dottie and I sat on the sofa, unsure of what to do next. The lady asked our names and where we lived. We answered, feeling stiff and awkward in this stranger's house. Some more questions—what grade are you in school? Do you like your teachers?

The other lady came back in the room bearing a silver tray with a pot of hot chocolate, cups, and a plate of cookies. She set it down, poured our hot chocolate and passed the cookies to us. We politely took one cookie.

"Sister, these young ladies are thirteen years old and are in the eighth grade. They live on Delphia Avenue."

"Oh, how nice. And do you have any hobbies? What do you like to do?"

Dottie and I were beginning to enjoy being treated like grown women at a tea party. We blossomed under this attention, drank our hot chocolate and had another cookie while we told the sisters what we liked to do, the books we were reading, the movies we liked, the ballroom dance lessons we were going to. Before we knew it, we had been there for an hour. It was curfew time.

We rose and thanked them. They made us promise to come visit again. We walked home wondering if Halloween was more fun the old way.

"Well, it's sure different," Dottie said.

"Uh huh. I sort of liked it," I admitted.

DOTTIE'S SECRET

On a sunny spring day after school, Dottie and I sat on my front porch trying to make an important decision. Dottie had been my best friend since fourth grade. Now, our graduation from eighth grade was approaching. The eighth-grade dance was coming up in three days, and the boys who had invited us to the dance were demanding an answer.

Dottie didn't like the boy who had asked her, and I didn't want to go with Warren. His mother and my mother were friends and I was suspicious that this date was arranged by them. Dottie and I preferred to go to the dance together and take our chances that we would be asked to dance by boys who came without dates. If we chose to do that, we knew we probably wouldn't dance at all because eighth grade boys would rather play baseball or do anything else except dance with girls. They would all stand around together across the room and laugh and punch each other but they wouldn't come near the girls.

I was perfectly happy to make that sacrifice rather than go with Warren. He always acted silly and moony around me. He named his horse, "Alice," after me and I didn't consider that a compliment.

So, when Dottie told me her mother said she should go to the dance with the boy who had invited her, I knew I was doomed to go as Warren's date. After we commiserated over our fate, Dottie told me she had a big secret to tell me.

I listened with disbelief while she told me she just found out she was adopted. Not only was she adopted, but her aunt and uncle who lived in Chicago were her real parents. That meant that all her cousins were really her brothers and sisters!

This was incredible! How could this happen? Who are the people she lives with whom she calls Mom and Dad? Did her cousins know she was their sister? Dottie and I had spent many summer days in her backyard hammock reading Nancy Drew mystery books, but none of them could compare to this mystery.

I didn't know anyone who was adopted. Maybe *I* was adopted—could I be adopted? I had a lot of cousins. Could they be my sisters and brothers? These questions raced through my mind.

Dottie told me her aunt and uncle came to her house last Sunday and told her they were her real mother and father. Then all her cousins hugged her and welcomed her as their little sister. Until now, she had been an only child. Her parents said now that she was thirteen years old, she was old enough to understand. They told her this story:

Dottie's real mother and father had nine children. When Dottie was born, they just couldn't afford another child. Dottie's aunt and uncle didn't have any children. They offered to take Dottie to live with them. Everyone was agreeable with this plan and the two families visited each other frequently. The nine siblings knew that Dottie was their sister but they were sworn to secrecy. It was unusual for nine children to keep such a secret.

Dottie's reaction to this revelation was unquestioned acceptance. Her love for her familiar "Mom" and "Dad" continued as strong as ever, but now she had another set of parents to love. I believe her loyalty remained with the parents she had lived with.

After I had assimilated this profound news, Dottie made another announcement that devastated me. Her aunt and uncle were going to move to Chicago to live close to her real parents so they could see each other every day. The move would take place during the summer so that Dottie would start high school in Chicago. In those days, high school started with ninth grade.

I was crushed! My best friend was moving away and I would start high school without her. I had other friends but Dottie was the one I shared all my thoughts and plans with.

During the past five years, we had packed sandwiches and rode our bikes to the forest preserves, stopped at the stables to feed apples to the horses, shopped for fabric and sewed doll clothes together and spent every summer day at the community pool except for the summers when all the pools and beaches in the Chicago area and suburbs were closed during the polio epidemic.

Polio (infantile paralysis) was spreading rapidly, crippling children and adults, even resulting in deaths. A special fund was started nationwide to provide money for research for the prevention and cure of polio. It was called "The March of Dimes." Jars were placed in school rooms, stores and offices. We brought dimes to put in the jars in school whenever our parents could spare some. President Franklin D. Roosevelt initiated the fund. He, himself, had polio and was in a wheelchair. In the 1950s a preventative vaccine was developed, and the dreaded virus was no longer a threat.

In the summers of the ban on public swimming, we visited the public library to check out all the Nancy Drew books. Dottie had a hammock in her backyard where we spent hours reading. Her parents worked in a bakery, and there were always day-old sweet rolls and cream puffs to munch on as we read. We also read all the Sue Barton, Student Nurse books and decided we were going to be nurses when we grew up. We had both just finished reading our first adult novel, "Gone With The Wind," and were fascinated with the search to find the perfect actress to play Scarlett O'Hara in the movie.

When we were ten years old and I had scarlet fever, I read almost all the Nancy Drew mystery books. There was nothing else to do. During that time, a building in town burned down to the ground. The investigators couldn't find a reason for the fire. I couldn't wait to get out of bed and solve that mystery with Dottie.

The day finally came when I was allowed out of the house and the red quarantine sign came off our front door. Dottie and I walked to the site of the building to search for clues. Sure enough, we found one. There, in the charred rubble, we found a shorthand notebook with shorthand writing in it. We walked to the police station, notebook in hand, and asked to see the chief of police. We were escorted to his desk and we proudly told him that we were on the verge of solving the mystery of the burned building.

The police chief listened to us attentively as I speculated that all the answers were in that shorthand notebook. I even offered my sister's services to decipher the writing because she was a secretary and could read shorthand. The police chief thanked us and said he would keep the notebook. He said it wasn't necessary for my sister to come in because he had a secretary. We walked out the door of that small police station, satisfied that we had helped solve a mystery.

Former Police Station and Town Hall

At the beginning of our eighth grade school year, dance lessons were offered after school in the gymnasium. It wasn't mandatory, but most of the boys were there because their mothers insisted they learn to dance. The girls attended because they loved to dance. Dottie and I attended the lessons regularly. I don't think there was a charge for the lessons.

We learned the Foxtrot, the waltz and the rumba. At first, we learned the steps individually until we knew them perfectly. Then, it was time to dance with partners. The boys groaned. Girls lined up against one wall of the gymnasium. The boys lined up directly across the room. At the instructor's signal, the boys walked across the room, each one found a girl, and said, "May I have this dance?" The girls then replied, "I'd be delighted."

When the music started, stiff-legged boys with sweaty palms held the girls in dance position and moved their feet. There was a great deal of struggling and toes being stepped on, but, eventually, we were actually enjoying the lessons.

On the days before the dance class, the girls usually discussed what they were going to wear to the class. One girl asked me, "What are you going to wear, Alice?" I didn't really have many choices but I really liked my "swing skirt." It was a skirt that fit snugly at the waist and hips, then flared out so that it was full at the hem at mid-knee length. It was fun to twirl around and see the bottom part flare.

"Oh, I think I'll wear my swing skirt."

"But you *always* wear your swing skirt," she said.

I didn't want to tell her I only had two dresses and a skirt and blouse. Dottie spoke up and said, "We *all* wear the same thing. Besides, Alice's skirt is beautiful." What a loyal friend!

We went to the eighth grade dance with our dates, and our graduation was celebrated by our respective families. I had my fourteenth birthday that summer of 1939. Dottie moved to Chicago and we swore eternal friendship. I started high school in September and made new friends.

Dottie, July 1939

Dottie and I occasionally spent weekends at each other's houses. I enjoyed the excitement of seeing all her brothers and sisters. Eventually, we grew apart but the memories of our years together remained in our hearts. Dottie followed her dream and became a nurse when she grew up.

THE OPEN ROAD

I had a girl friend named Joanne. The summer I turned fourteen, Joanne, her mother and I went on a ten day bicycle trip. I had saddlebags to keep my clothes, toothbrush, soap, washcloth and towel in. The saddlebags straddled the carrier on the back fender of my bike.

Joanne's mother had a map and a list of approved youth hostels where we could spend the nights. Youth hostel accommodations were usually on a farm. We slept on cots in barns or storage buildings for 50 cents a night. We were allowed to wash in the morning by using an old fashioned outdoor pump. We pumped the handle until water came out of the pipe. It was always ice cold, but we didn't mind. It was summertime and Illinois was hot in July.

Each morning we checked the map and planned how far we would travel that day. I don't remember much about what we did for meals, but they were simple and inexpensive. We probably stopped in a town for bread and lunchmeat to make sandwiches.

I put my blue and white Elgin bicycle to good use, pedaling past farms and forests on country roads. There were points of interest to stop by, and we went swimming whenever we came to a lake.

By the time we stopped for the night, we were so tired that the thin mattress on the cot felt fine, and we had no trouble falling into a deep sleep. A farmer's wife usually greeted us when we arrived to spend the night, but it was understood that she was not there to serve us. She showed us to the place we would bed down for the night, and then we were on our own. We were lucky if the bunk house had indoor plumbing, but most of the time we had to use the outhouse.

I had a sense of freedom as we passed unfamiliar places every day. Most of the time, we sang songs as we rode, sometimes making up our own words to old familiar songs. Joanne's mother was a good companion. She was born and grew up in Norway and had traveled like that in Europe.

On our last day, which was an especially hot day, we were getting thirsty and tired. It was noon and the sun beat down on us. We saw a large farm house ahead and decided to stop and ask for a drink of water. When we knocked on the door, the woman smiled and invited us to come in. We told her we just wanted a drink of water. She insisted, so we stepped inside her huge kitchen where about eight women were busily working over a stove and counter tops. Our hostess took us into an enormous dining room where at least twenty men in overalls were seated at a grand table, their plates heaped with food. She said, "Sit down, it's dinner time. These are our helpers. It's harvest time." Then she disappeared into the kitchen and Joanne, her mother and I looked at each other, not sure what to do.

Several women came in bearing bowls of mashed potatoes, fried chicken, and corn on the cob. They smiled and told us to sit down and eat. So, we obeyed, and had the best meal we had had in ten days. The women kept bringing more and more food and when I couldn't eat any more, they put pies in front of us. The men at the table were all jolly and joked with us. They were picking corn this week and had great appetites. Some of the men finished their meals and went back to the fields while others came in and sat down. There seemed to be a never ending flow of delicious food.

It was hard to pedal our bikes after that big meal, but we wanted to be home before nightfall so we persevered and arrived on time. I don't remember much about the places of interest we visited, but I will never forget the friendship and hospitality extended to three strangers.

Bicycle Tour

CHANGES

September 1939. The summer is ending. The days are still warm, but the early September evenings are cool. Leaves on the trees give us warnings that they will soon change color. There are big changes in everyone's lives. Dottie has moved to Chicago to start her new life. There is an empty feeling in my heart when I walk past her house. Life will never be the same.

I turned my thoughts to the "big day." In a few weeks I would leave my childhood behind and become a freshman in high school. My mother took me shopping for new school clothes and this time we shopped in the teen department. I sensed a change. Mom didn't have that "worried look" as we shopped. Unlike previous times, she let me choose clothes I really loved, and she didn't examine the price tags so carefully. She seemed to enjoy watching me make selections. She even bought me new shoes, and my old ones didn't have holes in them yet.

It seem like a heavy load has been lifted from the shoulders of my parents, aunts, uncles and neighbors. People are making plans for the future and buying new furniture and appliances. Our neighbor, Mr. Olson, was notified that he could start back to his old job. The Olson family and the Nelson family celebrated this occasion by going for a long walk around the neighborhood after supper, talking, laughing and even singing. The Depression was ending.

My figure is changing, too. It no longer looks boyish. My waist is smaller than my hips. There are no changes above my waist but only a few of my friends are developing in that way. I am getting taller—almost 5 feet 1 inch.

Newsreels at the movies are reporting on a war in Europe. I prayed that the princesses in England will be safe. During one of our Sunday dinners, Aunt Sadie and Aunt Tonie told my parents about some people who had escaped from Germany and are living next door to them in Chicago. They had some bad experiences and were lucky to get out of Germany. Mom excused me from the table after dessert was served, and, from the back porch, I could hear them talking in lowered voices about "how awful things were over there." I also learned a new word—"atrocities."

Our old turquoise Roosevelt car was traded in for a shiny new black Ford. During the first week in September, our family went on the first real vacation I could remember. We drove to Buffalo, New York in our new car to visit my oldest brother, Harold, and his wife, Alyce (spelled with a "y"), and my two nephews. It was so good to see Billy and Gene again. They were now seven and five years old and they claimed my attention during the visit. We saw Niagara Falls and ate dinners in restaurants.

Billy and Gene at Niagara Falls

For me, a change was coming that I never dreamed of. I was going to have a weekly *allowance*! I would be given one dollar every week. Fifty-five cents had to be used for a weekly bus ticket to go to high school but the rest, forty-five cents, was mine to spend.

I was rich!

GOODBYE, DOROTHY GREGORY

Shortly after we returned home from vacation, it was time for the big day. Maine Township High School was located two and one-half miles from our town, and it served two towns and their surrounding areas. There were forty-nine teachers and almost twelve hundred students in the 1939–1940 school year. This was a big change from Lincoln Elementary School where we knew all of our classmates and had known most of them since first grade.

I descended the steps of the school bus and followed the crowd into the beautiful enormous school. There were groups of students standing by their lockers, laughing and excited to see each other after the summer vacation. I noticed some of the boys were very tall and old enough to shave. Some of them looked almost like men. Everyone seemed to know where they were going as they walked through the halls.

Some teachers were assigned to greet the freshmen, look at their schedules, and point the way to their homerooms. Homeroom was reassuring. The teacher was friendly and quite a few of my friends were there.

Then the bell rang, and we left the room to find our individual classes. Boys and girls stood in groups chattering, then waved goodbye to each other and rushed off to their destinations. I glanced at my schedule and started walking, looking for the room number on the doors I passed but couldn't find the room I was assigned to. The halls were emptying and growing quiet. Most of the doors were closing. I had visions of walking into class late. How embarrassing!

Suddenly, an angel appeared. She was the most beautiful girl I had ever seen, and her eyes were full of compassion as she walked up to me. "Do you need help?" she asked. "I can't find this room," I said as I showed her my schedule. "I'll take you there," she said as she took my arm. "You'll get used to the numbers by the end of the day."

We hurried along and she introduced herself. "I'm Dorothy Gregory. What's your name?"

"Alice Nelson."

"Well, here's your classroom, Alice. Nice to meet you and good luck." She continued down the hall and I entered the room just a few seconds before the bell rang.

A few weeks later, I had the opportunity to talk with Dorothy Gregory and thank her for her kindness. She was a senior and she was planning for a career in radio after graduation. This was in 1939. Television would not be in family homes for thirteen more years. People listened to radio shows and Dorothy already had a job on a weekly radio program. She was allowed to leave classes early to go to the studio in Chicago for rehearsals and broadcasting.

National Honor Society member in her junior and senior years, class officer, president of the Girl's Club, beautiful in appearance and in spirit, Dorothy had a bright future ahead of her.

Dorothy didn't graduate from Maine Township High School. A few months before graduation day, Dorothy died of an aggressive type of leukemia.

That was seventy-three years ago, and I remember Dorothy and her kindness as if it were yesterday. A small gesture that meant so much to an anxious girl. In her short life, she fulfilled the destiny we are all on this earth for. We are here to love and help one another. You meet people like that throughout your lifetime. They show up to help you just when you are ready to give up hope.

Just consider this for a moment. A thoughtful word you have spoken or an act of kindness you have done for another person will be remembered forever.

How simple! How profound!

Dorothy Gregory

THEY ALSO REMEMBER

ED HOCH

We had an old Victrola that you wound up with a handle. We had thick Victor records. I remember some of the songs were, "The Wreck of the Old Ninety-Seven" and "Casey Jones." There was a pond near our house. We cut the ice from it in the winter and stored it in a shed with sawdust. That lasted us all summer for our ice box.

In the winter, we took baths in a metal tub in front of the stove in the kitchen. In the summer we went to the creek to bathe. We had no central heat.

My mother made skirts, pillow cases and dish towels from feed bags. They were pretty prints with flowers. We made dandelion wine with dandelion blossoms, oranges, raisins and sugar. We let it ferment until it was wine. We raised chickens for eggs. We were poor but we didn't know it.

BARBARA YINGLING

I remember my mother used old, worn-out stockings as curlers. They made those long, spiral curls.

JOAN HOCH

We lived in the country on a farm. There were only four houses on our road. It was too expensive to have wiring put in for electric service for so few houses, so we had no electricity. We had to read by the light of a kerosene lamp. We had a hand pump for water. My parents had our phone taken out because they couldn't afford it any more. My mother saved those bendable wires from the top of the bags of Eight O'Clock coffee and used them for hair curlers.

We raised hens, chickens and eggs, cows, ducks and turkeys. Once a week, on Friday, we loaded our truck and went to town to sell eggs. We raised all our food, including smoked hams and bacon. We made scrapple. The only things we had to buy at the store were flour, sugar and rice. We charged these things at the store and when our apples and potatoes were ready, and the store sold them, we paid our bill. Then the storekeeper gave my mother a bolt of fabric to make clothes for the children.

We had a good life. We didn't feel like we were poor.

ANONYMOUS

We didn't have many possessions but we had food, shelter and were warm in the winter. We played outside most of the time. We didn't have a sandpile, but we had a dirt pile. I made mud pies in the dirt pile and put cherries from our cherry tree in the "pies."

My father had built a small wooden trailer that he took up to the mountains when he was trapping. Most of the time, it just sat in our back yard under a tree and I used it for a play house. A young widow asked my parents if she could rent it to live in with her two small children. She paid five dollars a month. I don't know how they could fit in that small space.

BERNICE N. SOEFKER

We hung our laundry outside on a clothesline to dry. In the winter, the sheets would freeze and flip back and forth like huge pieces of cardboard. If it was raining or snowing the laundry was hung in the basement.

Spring break was the time to really clean the whole house. Even the attic floor was scrubbed. Windows and curtains were washed. Some of the curtains were put on curtain stretchers (those wood frames with sharp pin points to hold the curtains until they dried).

We did not have automatic water heaters. We had gas "sidearm" heaters. We lit the heater before doing the laundry or taking a bath and shut it off when we were done. Water for dishes was heated in a tea kettle.

We each had two pair of shoes: one pair for every day, and one pair for Sunday. When we wore a hole in the soles, Dad would buy a repair kit from the dime store. It consisted of a pair of rubber soles which could be trimmed to fit, a tube of glue, and a metal scraper to rough up the shoe soles to make the rubber sole adhere better.

Two of my friends and I would get outdated clothes pattern books from the dry goods store and make paper dolls from the pictures. We also played a lot of Monopoly.

Neighbors helped one another in so many ways. They shared with one another. They gave a helping hand to others when they were sick, and they all survived the Great Depression.

ANONYMOUS

We lived on the outskirts of a small town. There was no water or sewer service in our area so we had no running water. We had a pump outside of the house and we had an outhouse. I remember a card my mother would put in the window for the ice man. It showed how many pounds of ice you wanted him to cut for your ice box. The ice man would cut the ice into a big cube with an ice pick and he gave all the kids chips of ice to chew on.

SHIRLEY LEOPOLD

Our meals were simple but we didn't go hungry. On rainy days, my father was able to drive us home from school because his work hours had been cut back.

JEANNE CRONE

It cost twenty-five cents for an adult ticket to the movies, but on Tuesday nights, you could buy a ticket for ten cents and you were given a free dish. Some people were able to acquire an entire dinnerware set just by going to the movies on Tuesday nights. I remember hearing dishes crashing on the floor during the movies because people held them on their laps and forgot about them while watching the movie, and the plates would slide off their laps.

You would find a small green bowl inside an oatmeal box. Sometimes there would be a green glass. I still have some of those. I have seen them in antique stores selling for thirty-five dollars. Boxes of soap powder had dish towels inside. All of these free prizes were marketing techniques to get people to buy their brand.

Oatmeal Box Glassware

Jeanne Crone's mother passed away when Jeanne was six years old, and her sister was four years old. Her father was an automotive repair man. He and the two girls lived in an apartment above the shop. The following stories are memories written by Jeanne Crone:

Friendship and a One Dollar Bill. Perhaps Barney's first visit to my father's shop was for business as both men dealt with automobiles. Bill, my father, repaired automotive electrical systems, rebuilt generators, ground valves and did any work to restore a car to good running condition. Barney, together with his brother, operated an auto graveyard and was my father's source of used car parts.

As time passed, Barney stopped into the shop to talk and the friendship of the two men grew. "You don't seem happy today," my father told his friend. "There's just no money around, Bill," stated Barney. "I haven't even got one dollar."

"Yeah, I know. Things sure are lean everywhere. This Depression is hitting everyone hard," agreed my father.

"But my trouble is," continued the younger man, "I have a date with this great girl, Minnie. How can I make a good impression on her if I can't even buy her an ice cream cone? Where can I take her without any money at all?"

"Isn't there something you can do? Perhaps you can take a walk?" suggested my father. "Sure, but she's always had it good, and I want to make a lasting impression on her. How can I do it without a cent? My brother can't loan me a buck. We're stone broke!" he complained.

My father reached into his pocket, withdrawing his wallet. "No, no, Bill," the excited young man exclaimed. I wasn't asking for a loan from you. You've got your family to take care of."

"Here," he said as he withdrew one of the two dollars in his wallet. "No, no," Barney insisted, embarrassed that his friend might think he was hinting for a loan. "Besides, I couldn't pay it back for a long time."

"This isn't a loan. It's *your* dollar to take your girl on a date. Take it and have a good time!" my father answered. As Barney held the money in his hand and walked through the shop door, he looked back at his benefactor and promised, "Bill, I'll never forget you. This dollar will return to you a thousand times."

Throughout their friendship over the years, whenever one of the men needed something the other had, it was given without any money exchange, regardless of value. Favors passed between the two men regularly, keeping alive the promise given over three decades ago.

More Memories from Jeanne Crone. There was a church seven blocks away from our house that showed movies on Fridays at six o'clock, and it only cost two cents. If you didn't have two cents, you could get in for one cent. I remember going at five-thirty to be in line and talk with the kids until it opened. I was glad to be there in line. Nowadays, I can hardly imagine that I was allowed to walk there alone and return home after dark. It was a time when everyone looked out for children.

The movies at the church were a good thing, a way to entertain children that otherwise had nothing to do. Sometimes, kids with no penny begged someone in line for one cent.

The daughter of the owner of the large department store had taken music lessons and played the piano. At the end of the season, they had a recital. It was published in the newspaper that anyone who wanted to could come to the store and hear her play the music she had learned.

On the way home from the two-cent movie, I saw the people going to the store, which usually closed at six o'clock. It was now seven-thirty. So, I went in too, and sat on a chair. The fabric department of the store was the location of the concert. The tables and merchandise were moved into another department, and chairs that were borrowed from an undertaker were set in rows.

Beside me sat a nice young lady with a three-year-old boy. She asked, "Are you alone?"

"Yes," I replied, not thinking it was unusual. "Where is your mother?"

she asked. I could hardly talk. Choked up, I said, "My mother is dead. She died last year." Her arms were around me immediately, and tears flowed down our cheeks as the music began.

At that time, I realized what I was missing—the love that a child really needs from a mother.

One dark night, there was a parade. It was unusual. There was no band, no uniforms other than their old, worn clothing. Men and boys and a few women marched through the entire town of Allentown, which was much smaller than it is now. They tooted whistles and beat makeshift drums and carried signs that read: "Help Us!" "My Kids Are Hungry," and "God, Where Are You?" My father took offense at that sign. How can you blame God for all the trouble in the world?

They were people everyone knew. I saw the man from our neighborhood who had two daughters. He was a second generation American from Italy. With his wife and two children, he lived in a broken down apartment above a shop, just as we did.

One very cold, wintry day, a year after my mother died, a lady came into the shop. Her car had stopped, and she couldn't start it. She asked my dad to come and start it so she could get to her job. She took care of an old man who lived on Fifth Street. My father got the car started, but something else started—a romance. They seemed to need each other. She, having been divorced. He, a widower. Her daughter, Shirley, was in my class in second grade.

They were married on June 30 of that year. Now, I had another sister, Shirley. It was sort of embarrassing to explain how this all happened. My teachers knew my mother had died. I think they understood how a man feels trying to take care of little girls and work too.

Our new mother tried very hard to be our mother, but she lacked the real motherly love we needed.

The Player Piano. The upright player piano stood in the living room of the small apartment we lived in. It was directly above my father's shop. Almost constantly, someone was on the piano bench, pumping the foot pedals as the piano roll played. As soon as one of us tired of playing, there were two more girls waiting to pump away.

The roll of paper, cut with a pattern of holes, moved across a brass bar that had openings corresponding to the keys on the piano. As the pattern crossed a note, air passed through and that particular note was struck. If we wanted to play the music faster, we pumped the pedals faster. As time went on, we developed many variations as we played the familiar songs over and over again. Many of these were war songs of the 1918 vintage, but there were a few old hymns recorded with extra trills and musical embellishments.

"Don't you ever give that piano a rest?" asked my stepmother, noticeably annoyed by the constant music.

"No, it's fun to play it," was our stock reply.

"Well, I'm sick of hearing the same tunes constantly. Can't you play anything else?"

"We've played all the rolls that are in good enough condition to use," I told her, motioning to the box which held the long black containers of piano rolls. "The others are too brittle, are torn, and some have come off the wooden rollers."

As she went on her way, disgusted by the ceaseless sounds, she muttered something like, "Well, at least they aren't fighting."

I have an idea," Doris said. "Let's make our own piano roll and surprise mother."

"Yeah," agreed Shirley. "We could surprise her with some really different music."

"It will be different, all right," I laughed. "We don't know exactly where to put the holes and the notes will play without order."

"C'mon, let's try it," urged Doris, excitedly.

Shirley suggested, "We could use an old window shade in the closet."

"No, that would be too bulky," I told my eager sisters. "Shelf paper would move along better. There's a new roll in the kitchen cabinet." I explained. "I was supposed to line the shelves with it. I'm sure we can use that."

"We can't ask Mother for it. That'd spoil the surprise," said Shirley.

Doris returned from the kitchen carrying the roll of white paper. "It's twice as wide as the player rolls," she said as she compared the shelf paper to the piano roll.

"We'll have to cut it to the right size first," answered Shirley.

"I'll get a scissors and we can begin while mother is busy," I said as I hurried away.

The shelf paper was spread out on the table. Lines were measured and drawn the entire length of the roll of paper. Shirley walked along one side cutting away the excess paper. Suddenly she said, "We could make our composition twice as long if we trim off the larger half and glue it together."

"Wow," remarked Doris. "We'll have a full-sized long-playing piano roll."

After the paper was cut to size, with a punch and hammer, we marked and punctured the surface, being careful to put a board under it to protect the table. "This is too slow for me," announced my impatient little sister as she waited her turn to make holes in the paper. "I'd like to do my own notes. I want to do the middle notes."

"Okay, you can," agreed Shirley. "I'll get the ice pick and do the high notes."

"I like the bass notes the best anyway, so I'll do them," I said as all three of us marked and cut patterns of holes into the paper.

"If I know anything about music, this is going to sound sort of awful," Shirley told us.

"Put some holes here," Doris suggested, pointing to blank spaces on my side of the paper. It looks kind of bare here."

"Look," Doris announced proudly, "I've made the scales run up and down."

"Hey, that does look nice," I said, admiring my younger sister's efforts. "But the test is how will it sound?"

"As soon as the glue dries, I'd like to be the person to play it first," Shirley said as she pasted the wooden rolls to the ends of the paper.

"What will we name our new piano roll?" asked Doris.

"Oh," I answered quickly, "We can't name it until we hear it."

At last, the time came to listen to our masterpiece. With pomp and ceremony, Shirley took her place on the bench as we watched with interest. It was not unexpected, but the ultimate symphony of discordant notes was simply unbelievable. Series of bangs on the low notes were interrupted by tingling bangs on the high notes, while the middle notes played makeshift scales, missing a note or striking several simultaneously.

"This is really awful," Doris admitted as she made faces at the piano. "Listening to this is like punishment."

"That's it," I told them excitedly. "We'll call it *Chastisement.*That's a little worse than punishment."

Mother heard the cacophony of noises and came running. "Who is banging on the piano?" she shouted.

"No one," we replied innocently, as Shirley smugly pumped away.

"We made our very own piano roll," proudly announced Doris.

"And we've named it Chastisement," I volunteered, "Because it's like being punished to listen to it."

Then Mother laughed at our inventive project, but when we played it repeatedly, the sounds annoyed her. Do you suppose she had anything to do with our piano roll's sudden and mysterious disappearance?

Piano Roll Production
Sketch by Jean Grimm

INDEX